Wonderful Wraps

Wonderful Wraps

MAKE YOUR GIFTS MEAN EVEN MORE

Marie Browning

Sterling Publishing Co., Inc.

New York

Prolific Impressions Production Staff:

Editor in Chief: Mickey Baskett
Copy Editor: Phyllis Mueller
Graphics: Dianne Miller, Karen Turpin
Styling: Kirsten Jones
Photography: Jerry Mucklow
Administration: Jim Baskett

Library of Congress Cataloging-in-Publication Data Available

10 9 8 7 6 5 4 3 2 1

2003002679

Published in paperback 2004 by Sterling Publishing Co., Inc.
387 Park Avenue South, New York, N.Y. 10016

© 2003 by Prolific Impressions, Inc.

Produced by Prolific Impressions, Inc.
160 South Candler St., Decatur, GA 30030

Distributed in Canada by Sterling Publishing
c/o Canadian Manda Group, One Atlantic Avenue, Suite 105
Toronto, Ontario, Canada M6K 3E7
Distributed in Great Britain by Chrysalis Books Group PLC
The Chrysalis Building, Bramley Road, London W10 6SP, England
Distributed in Australia by Capricorn Link (Australia) Pty. Ltd.
P.O. Box 704, Windsor, NSW 2756 Australia

Printed in China
All rights reserved

Sterling ISBN 1-4027-0344-9 Hardcover
        ISBN 1-4027-1774-1 Paperback

Acknowledgements

Accu-Cut Systems
Fremont, NE, USA
www.accucut.com
Die cut shapes and personal cutting and scoring template systems

American Art Clay Co., Inc.
Indianapolis, IN, USA
www.amaco.com
Polymer clay

Bayley's Boxes
Black Hawk, CO, USA
www.bayleysboxes.com
Flat box blanks in many styles and shapes

Boutique Trims, Inc.
South Lyon, MI, USA
www.boutiquetrims.com
Large selection of charms in many finishes, including antiqued gold, patina, and copper

Fiskars Inc.
Wausau, WI, USA
www.fiskars.com
Art knives, hand drill, paper trimmers, cutting mats, rotary cutter, decorative edge scissors

Magenta Art Stamps
Ste. Julie, Quebec, Canada
www.magentarubberstamps.com
Flat box blanks in many styles and shapes, art stamps and stamp accessories

Plaid Enterprises Inc.
Norcross, GA, USA
www.plaidonline.com
Acrylic craft paints, decoupage finish, fabric paint

About Marie Browning

Pressed Flower Gallery
San Marino, CA, USA
www.pressedflower.com
Pressed flowers, stickers

Quilting Creations
International Inc.
Zoar, OH, USA
www.quiltingcreations.com
Package and box stencil templates

Xyron, Inc.
Scottsdale, AZ, USA
www.xyron.com
*Adhesive application and
laminating machines*

*Decorative papers, handmade
papers, card paper, and stickers were
provided by the following
companies:*
K & Company
Parkville, MO, USA
www.Kandcompany.com

Papers by Catherine
Houston, TX, USA
www.papersbycatherine.com

Petersen-Arne
Eugene, OR, USA
www.petersenarne.com

Treasure Mart
Richmond, BC, Canada
www.treasuremart.net

Marie Browning is a consummate craft designer who has made a career of designing products, writing books and articles, and teaching and demonstrating. You may have been charmed by her creative acumen but not been aware of the woman behind it; she has designed stencils, stamps, transfers, and a variety of other products for art and craft supply companies.

She is the author of four books on soapmaking: *Designer Soaps* (Sterling 2003), *300 Handcrafted Soaps* (Sterling 2002), *Beautiful Handmade Natural Soaps* (Sterling, 1998) and *Melt & Pour Soapmaking* (Sterling, 2000). In addition to books about soapmaking, Browning has authored three other books published by Sterling: *Jazzy Jars* (2002), *Handcrafted Journals, Albums, Scrapbooks & More* (1999), *Making Glorious Gifts from Your Garden* (1999), *Crafting with Vellum & Parchment* (2001), *Memory Gifts* (2000). Her articles and designs have appeared in *Better Homes & Gardens, Great American Crafts, All American Crafts, Crafts, Craftworks,* and in numerous project books published by Plaid Enterprises, Inc.

Marie Browning earned a Fine Arts Diploma from Camosun College and attended the University of Victoria. She is a Certified Professional Demonstrator, a professional affiliate of the Canadian Craft and Hobby Association, and a member of the Stencil Artisans League and the Society of Craft Designers.

She lives, gardens, and crafts on Vancouver Island in Canada. She and her husband Scott have three children: Katelyn, Lena, and Jonathan. Marie can be contacted at www.mariebrowning.com ❏

Contents

8 INTRODUCTION

10 PACKAGE MAKING & DECORATING MATERIALS

24 BASIC PACKAGING TECHNIQUES

24 DECORATING TECHNIQUES

38 FINISHING TOUCHES

46 HOW TO COVER A BOX

50 MAKING GIFT BOXES

52 Quick Box

54 Square Box

56 Origami Box

60 Collapsible Box

63 Match Box

64 Shaped Boxes

66 Pyramid Boxes

68 Cornucopia Box

72 Pillow Pouch

74 Pointed Paper Pouch

77 Interlocking Box

78 Paper Purse

79 Column Twist Container

82 Triangle Long Box

84 Fold-Over Package

88 Teabag-style Package

90 Envelope Pouch

92 Traditional Christmas Crackers

94 MAKING GIFT BAGS

96 Tall Gift Bag

97 Quick Bag Favors

98 La Petite Purse

100 Bag Toppers

102 Accordion Top Bag

104 BEYOND PAPER

105 Metal Packages

107 Plastic Containers

110 Fabric Bags & Pouches

112 Cellophane Wrapping

114 Terra Cotta Pot Packages

Making your own decorative packages is rewarding and fun. Here are a variety of designs and techniques, both simple and complex, for making beautiful boxes and bags. I have offered my favorites and my best no-fail hints for assembling and decorating them with ease. The materials and equipment are generally inexpensive, and artistic skills are not required! Whether you are making a gift bag from decorative paper, recycling a box with decoupage or painting techniques, or decorating a plastic bottle or a terra cotta pot, the package for your gift will mean more if you make it yourself. Inventive packaging is also an important component of selling handmade products like herb mixes, bath salts, and handcrafted jewelry and ornaments – they'll fly off the shelves at craft fairs or gift stores when you spend some time on the presentation.

The package for your gift will mean more if you make it yourself.

Simple instructions and an assortment of patterns are provided to guide you through a multitude of creative ideas, from quick and easy packages to ornate decorative presentations. You can further accent your packages with metal charms, ribbons, lace, buttons, shells, and a host of other embellishments. The photographs show dozens of ideas for accenting.

In this book, you'll see how you can create and decorate unique boxes and bags that are the best gift of all – your time and creativity. Enjoy!

Marie Browning

Package Making & Decorating Materials

THIS SECTION INTRODUCES THE MATERIALS you'll use to create beautiful packages – various kinds of papers, purchased bags and boxes, and ribbons, cords, and twine for embellishing and fastening – and the equipment you'll use for constructing them – templates, markers, adhesives, and tools for cutting and folding.

Paper

Paper is all around us, made by machine and by hand, available in an infinite number of thicknesses, weights, textures, colors, and patterns. You can make packages from papers you purchase or from papers that you have decorated.

Papers are manufactured in standard sizes and weights. Often a paper is identified by the weight of a ream (500 sheets) that has been cut to a given size. Lower weight papers are lighter and thinner. For example, a piece of paper for photocopying is usually a 20-lb. paper, while a business card might be made of a 60-lb. paper.

Below: Printed and embossed papers are available at most craft and hobby stores in a wide range of designs

◆ Card Paper or Card Stock

This is the main paper used for box and parcel construction. A 40-lb. to 60-lb. weight card paper will make sturdy boxes up to 8" long. For larger boxes, you will need a heavier paper such as bristle board.

Card paper is available in standard letter-size sheets (8-1/2" x 11") and the larger 12" x 12" size. These are the standard paper sizes for the scrapbooking industry, and they are easy to find at craft stores and paper outlets. Because the art of scrapbooking has become so popular in recent years, there is a huge selection of beautiful patterned and colored theme papers available. For larger projects that require heavier paper, poster-size card is available from art supply outlets.

◆ Decorative Papers

Along with wrapping paper, origami paper, and decoupage paper, there are lighter weight papers in an infinite number of colors, patterns, and themes in 8-1/2" x 11" and 12" x 12" sizes. The lighter weights of these papers are fine for the smaller parcels, decorative labels, and simple folded packages. If you find a beautiful lighter weight paper you want to use for a larger box, simply follow the instructions for laminating the paper to a piece of heavier card paper.

Shown here is a variety of handmade papers and specialty papers. A photocopy of a photograph printed on a specialty paper makes great package making paper.

◆ Handmade Paper

The soft, fabric-like qualities of handmade paper make it perfect for covering boxes and for making folded containers such as the fold-over pouch, collapsible box, and pointed pouch. Handmade paper has a deckle edge on all sides. It is available from all over the world and is made from a great variety of plant fibers – there is the more familiar rice paper, as well as

paper made with silk, straw, and mulberry. (Even papers made from elephant dung are available.)

Handmade papers come in a variety of weights, but the most-used are the text weight, which is good for covering boxes, and cover weight, which is used for parcel construction. Fine, lightweight handmade paper is easy to laminate to heavier card paper for parcels that require a firmer paper.

Handmade papers are available in a great many thicknesses, colors, and designs. Standard-size sheets (8-1/2" x 11") are available at craft stores and scrapbooking supply outlets. Larger sheets (20" x 30") can be found at quality paper stores and art supply outlets.

◆ Suede Paper

This soft-textured paper is available in many colors, in mottled animal print patterns, and embossed. The fuzzy surface of suede paper can be decorated with rubber stamps or stencils. Because the backside is smooth, suede paper is easy to cut and adhere to projects. I mainly use it for lining boxes, but it also can be used for package construction after laminating it to a heavier, firmer paper.

◆ Vellum and Parchment Paper

Crisp parchment and vellum are strong enough to hold up to package construction, and they hold clean, crisp folds. The beauty of the paper's smooth, translucent surface gives the package a glowing effect.

Care must be taken when working with these papers, but you'll be successful if you follow the instructions in the techniques section. Many adhesives show through parchment and vellum, and special care must be taken when scoring and folding so the paper doesn't crack or split.

There is a wide selection of vellum and parchment papers available; they are generally very light in weight and translucent. A large selection of patterned, colored, and embossed vellums and parchment are available in 8-1/2" x 11" and 12" x 12" sheets.

◆ Tissue Paper

Plain or patterned tissue paper can be used for constructing packages if it is laminated on heavier card. The faux leather decorative treatment uses the thinness of tissue paper to achieve texture.

OTHER PAPER IDEAS

- **Sheets of sandpaper** give a great look to pyramid boxes or sea theme packages decorated with shells. Sandpaper is available in many different grades of texture and shades of beige, black, and sand. Instead of an art knife or slide cutter, use an old pair of scissors to cut sandpaper – it will help sharpen the scissors!

- **Clear plastic sheets** are great for making packages that show off the contents, so they're a perfect choice for potpourri, colored bath salts, or spice blends. (If you wish to hide the gift, you can place it in a bed of crinkled paper basket filler or wood excelsior in the clear package.) Clear plastic sheets also are used for covering windows in packages. They are easy to cut, score, and fold, but care must be taken when assembling the package as all adhesives show through and some will melt or warp the plastic. (Double-sided cellophane tape works best for holding the package together.)

- **Photographs** enlarged on a color photocopier or scanned and printed make wonderful personal packages. Top quality copy paper, which is a little bit heavier, is used to create these charming "memory packages."

- **Heavier mat board** can be used to make larger boxes – I used it for the tops and bottoms of shaped boxes.

◆ Flat Box Blanks

Flat box blanks are great surfaces for decorating. You can paint, sponge, stamp, or cover them with decorative paper or fabric while flat and then assemble them to create your own unique packages. You also can find exceptional shapes and designs that would be difficult to cut out yourself. Craft stores, rubber-stamping stores, packaging and container stores, kitchen stores, and candy supply outlets are places to look for boxes.

◆ Gift Bags

Kraft paper lunch bags, white and colored bags of all sizes, and patterned and metallic bags can be used to create exciting packages. Using paper bags is economical; several fun and quick ideas are offered. This book offers ways to jazz up plain gift bags to make them beautiful and personal.

◆ Stencil Templates and Die-cut Packages

You can buy stencil templates that allow you to use your own decorative papers to make custom packages. They are easy to use, but you are, however, limited to the sizes and shapes offered.

You also can have package designs cut from your choice of papers at stores that offer a die-cut system. Die-cut packages are cut by machines and come in shapes that would be difficult to cut yourself. Many scrapbooking stores offer this service for their customers.

◆ Other Boxes

Blank papier mache and cardboard boxes also are available in many sizes and shapes, ready to decorate. Don't forget that boxes can be easily reused and decorated.

◆ Beyond Paper

Tins, frosty plastic boxes and bags, clear plastic jars and bottles, fabric pouches, and even clay pots make wonderful containers for gifts and for presenting homemade treasures. Find them at card shops, container and packaging stores, and garden centers.

Equipment

These are the basic items necessary to create simple handmade packages. The projects in this book require simple tools that are easily accessible and essential for successful construction.

◆ Cutting Tools

- **Scalpel-type art knife** or **craft knife** with a replaceable, pointed blade is essential. It's an all-purpose cutting knife for different types of papers. Scissors won't give you the straight, sharp edges that are essential for successful packages. Be sure to have a supply of additional blades to ensure you'll always have a sharp cutting edge.

- **Cutting mat** that is self-healing with a printed grid protects your work surface and provides very accurate cuts. The mat surface seals itself after each cut, so your knife won't follow a previous cut. The mats with 1", 1/2", and 1/4" grid markings make measuring and cutting perfectly square corners a breeze. Cutting mats range in size from 9" x 12" to mats that will cover an entire tabletop. Buy the biggest mat your budget will allow. You must use a cutting mat when using a rotary cutter or you will damage the blade.

A shape template and a cutter

- **Straight-edge metal ruler** with a cork backing is needed for perfectly straight cuts. Wooden and plastic rulers will slide, and your knife will cut into them. Lengths from 12" to 18" long are useful for paper parcel projects.

- **Paper trimmer with a sliding blade** is useful for general cutting – you can use an art knife instead, but a paper trimmer makes the job much easier and faster. Paper trimmers are excellent for cutting precise panels for covering boxes and for creating your own double-sided tape from double-sided adhesive sheets. They are more available to home crafters now because prices have come down.

- **Craft scissors** are needed for cutting small pieces of paper, decorative treatments like ribbons, and labels. Small sharp scissors also are needed for cutting out images for decoupage.

- **Decorative edge scissors** are a must for paper crafting. Their different decorative edges give just the right finishing touch.

- **Rotary cutter** can cut through several layers of card or fabric with ease and create perfect, straight edges. It is also useful for cutting handmade paper, as an art knife tends to tear lighter papers made with fibers and botanicals.

- **Shape templates and shape cutters** (also known as personal die-cutting systems) are a new way to cut your own professional-looking shapes. The shapes make attractive, professional-looking labels and the system is perfect for making shaped windows in parcels easily and quickly. Shape templates are available in a wide selection of motifs, letters, and numbers and as package and envelope templates.

- **Hole punches** are useful for making holes before setting eyelets and holes for threading cords and decorative threads into packages. **Shaped paper punches** add decorative touches to parcel designs and can be used for cutouts, borders, and design elements.

◆ Folding Tools

• **Embossing tools** with small ball ends are useful for scoring when using a stencil template. (A bone folder is generally too thick to fit in the guide lines.) Embossing tools are also useful for scoring vellum and parchment papers where a bone folder proves to be too thick. I also use it for marking paper so there is no need to erase a pencil line.

• **Bone folder** is used to fold sharp creases, score fold lines, and to help smooth papers when adhering them to a surface. A bone folder does not bruise or scratch paper when used for folding, as a plastic folder tends to do. An 8" bone folder with a pointed end is convenient for general work. If you are unable to find a bone folder, substitute a dull kitchen knife for scoring.

Adhesives

Using the proper adhesive is important for successful projects. An adhesive should be able to hold the paper together but not seep through. You want embellishments to adhere tightly to your packages, even if mailed or handled roughly.

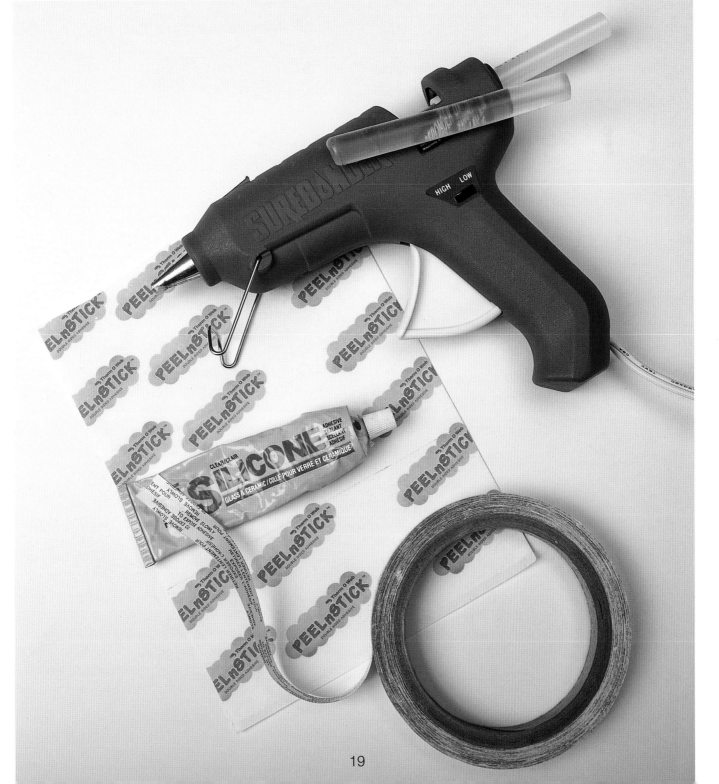

◆ Glue Stick

For paper, a glue stick – solid glue in a stick form – is convenient and simple to use. Use glue sticks that are non-toxic and acid free for laminating papers, gluing labels, and basic parcel building.

◆ Craft Glue

Thick, tacky craft glue is used for adhering heavier papers together and gluing on decorative trims and accents such as metal charms and trims.

◆ Hot Glue Guns

Hot glue guns and glue sticks are much quicker to use than white craft glue – pieces stick together immediately. However, there's no opportunity for re-positioning or removal if something is glued in the wrong position. Use high temperature glue for strong bonds; crystal clear sticks are not visible under translucent papers.

◆ Spray Adhesives

Spray adhesive works well for laminating large pieces of paper together. Have a separate, well-ventilated area for spraying the piece and protect the surrounding area well. This glue is very sticky and can be messy to work with.

◆ Decoupage Finish

Acrylic decoupage finish is useful for laminating papers together and for creating decorative treatments such as faux leather and decoupage. It can also be used for pasting decorative papers to boxes. It goes on smoothly and evenly and dries clear. Be aware that it will seep through finer handmade papers.

◆ Double-Sided Adhesive Products

• **Double-sided adhesive sheets** (also called mounting adhesive) are perfect for laminating papers together. Because the adhesive completely covers the area with an even coating of sticky film, the results are strong and invisible under fine handmade papers and vellum papers. The sticky film adds no moisture (as glues do) so the paper won't wrinkle or warp.

• **Double-sided tapes** are used to adhere package seams and for the gold leaf striping decorating technique. The tapes are strong and adhere instantly for quick package construction. Double-sided tape is available in a variety of widths, from 1/4" to 3/4". Roller-type tape dispensers are available for applying double-sided tape.

• You can also create your own custom-width double-sided tape by cutting sheets of mounting adhesive – use a slide cutter to cut the sheets to the exact width you need.

• Use **double-sided foam tape** for creating a raised effect for embellishments.

◆ Laminating Adhesive Products

• **Iron-On fusible adhesive** works well for laminating lighter papers to heavier card paper, and it is the best adhesive for laminating fabric to paper. The bond is strong and the edges are fused, so fabric won't unravel and there's no glue to seep through. The "ultra-hold" strength is best for package construction. Find it at crafts and fabric stores. *Always* follow the manufacturer's instructions and use a pressing cloth or pressing paper to protect your iron and work surface when laminating with a fusible adhesive.

• **Laminating film** is a clear, flexible adhesive film that is sticky on only one side. It can be used to laminate pressed flowers, feathers, and paper images. I also like to laminate paper templates for extra strength and longevity. Laminating film is available in large sheets or small panels in finishes from shiny to matte. To use, simply peel away the backing paper and apply. Try **clear shipping labels** for smaller laminating jobs.

• **Adhesive application and laminating machines** instantly apply an adhesive to whole sheets of paper for quickly laminating two papers together. The machines also can turn paper motifs into stickers without using heat or moisture, instantly apply single or double-sided polypropylene laminate to papers, or create decorative magnets for tin containers. Changeable cartridges allow you to apply permanent adhesive (best for package making), repositionable adhesive, plastic sheet on one side and adhesive on the other, double-sided plastic laminate, plastic laminate, and sheet magnet. They are simple, quick, and worth the expense for the time

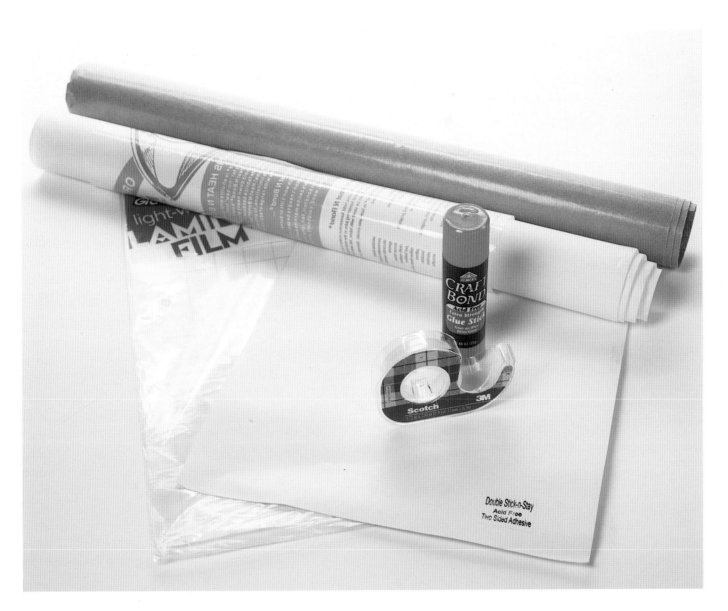

saved. After you use one of these machines, you will wonder how you managed without it!

- You can laminate fine papers, pressed leaves, or tissue to **freezer paper** with a hot iron to make a sturdy paper. To laminate, place your fine paper on the shiny side of the freezer paper. With a hot iron and no steam, press the papers together. The plastic coating of the freezer paper will melt, adhering the papers. Freezer paper comes on rolls and you can find it in grocery stores. For a lovely effect, place pressed flowers between freezer paper and thin rice paper to laminate them within the two papers. Freezer paper is also handy for protecting your work surface.

Decorating Materials

After you have your box or bag constructed, there are a number of ways to decorate it. Following are some easy to find materials that can be used to enhance your package simply and easily. In the "Decorating Techniques" chapter are even more supplies you can use to add special touches to your packages.

◆ Ribbon, Cord & Twine

Many types of cords, ribbons, and twines can be used to decorate and fasten packages. Thinner widths are easier to thread through the holes; wider ribbons can be used for decorative effect. Examples include natural raffia, satin ribbon, sheer ribbon, grosgrain ribbon, decorative fibers, jute, elastic cord, and garden twine.

◆ Markers

• **Air-erase pens** are great for tracing marks and lines on paper – the marks fade away in 24 to 48 hours. Be sure to purchase an air-erase, *not* a water-erase pen when working on paper. Find them in fabric or scrapbooking departments of crafts stores.

• You can also use a **pencil** for marking. If you do, draw the lines so they will be easier to erase. You can also use a bone folder; if you do, there is no line to erase but embossed marks are harder to see so make sure your work area is well lighted.

• Try **colored felt-tip pens**, **calligraphy pens**, **gel pens**, and **paint markers** for decorative treatments and writing on the labels.

22

◆ Fasteners

Fasteners are the decorative and functional closures for packages – you may find them to be the main decorative element of a package. Generally, it's best to select a fastener that's easily removable, so the recipient can retrieve the gift without damaging the parcel.

Here are a few fun ideas:

- **Wooden clothespins** are a nice choice for a quaint homemade look whether you use standard spring pins, miniature pins, or old-fashioned pins.

- **Eyelets** are available in many colors, sizes, and shapes. Use them to reinforce holes or accent a package.

- **Buttons** and **Chinese coins** can be laced with cord – the variety available is enormous.

- **Brads** (also called paper fasteners and split pins) are inexpensive – learn how to make brads different colors in the techniques section.

- **Wire clips**, from ordinary paper clips to swirl-shaped Italian paper clips and ones you can make yourself, are excellent closures.

- **Hook-and-loop dots** are useful for making concealed closures. They are easy to attach to fabric pouches, paper purses, and fold-over packages.

◆ Embellishments

Embellishments are the accents that give your packages character and interest. The variety of accents available is huge; here are some of my favorites:

- **Silk flowers** are inexpensive and readily obtainable. They look especially nice glued on fabric pouches.

- Ribbon roses, metal charms, and buttons are easy to find and come in a great number of motifs and colors. When gluing heavy objects such as charms, use thick, tacky craft glue for best results.

- Beads can be used to adorn cords. Tiny glass marbles can be used on fabric and plastic containers.

- Gold leaf gilding can be a stunning accent, and I've included an easy tape method.

- Stickers are about the easiest to use and find, and they are available in an enormous variety to accent any theme. Pressed flower stickers, lettering stickers, and embossed stickers designed to match decorative papers are also available. Tips for making your own stickers are in the technique section.

- Eyelets can be used to reinforce holes for ribbon or cording or as an accent.

Basic Packaging Techniques

TO BE SUCCESSFUL WITH THE PROJECTS in this book, you'll need to learn a few basic techniques. Cutting clean, straight lines; folding sharp, crisp creases; measuring accurately, and gluing flaps perfectly are all important skills for making your own packages. These skills are easy to master with practice and the proper tools.

Cutting

Cutting with an art knife is an important skill when working with paper. Because many people don't cut correctly, I offer these tips:

- The key to successful cutting with an art knife is having a good sharp blade. Always have extra blades handy so your knife is in top cutting form. It is safer to use a sharp blade than a dull blade, which can easily slip.

- To cut straight lines, use a metal ruler as a guide. Hold down the ruler firmly with your non-cutting hand, and keep that hand on the ruler until you've completed the cut. Be safe – keep your fingers well back on the ruler and out of the path of the blade to avoid accidents.

- Use the grid markings on your cutting mat for measuring and lining up the paper while cutting. If you do, you won't need to make as many marks on your paper and your corners will be perfectly square.

Cutting with an art knife

• Hold the art knife like a pen, with your index finger (it's your strongest) on top of the handle. Make sure the blade is held at a constant, low angle to the paper, and make strong, one-motion cuts towards you. You'll make cleaner cuts by exerting a downward pressure on the blade while cutting, but don't press too hard – you could rip the paper.

• When cutting through heavy card paper, don't try to cut it all in one go – use two or three consistent strokes with firm pressure, and the card paper will cut easily. Use this same technique when cutting through a stack of papers. Hold the ruler firmly and make as many cuts as needed to penetrate all the layers. • Always measure twice and cut once.

Folding

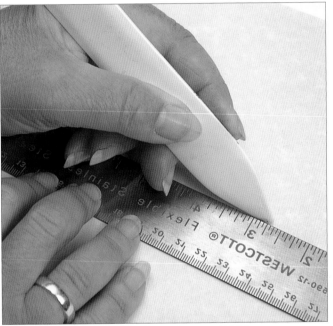

Score with a bone folder to emboss a fold line.

Clean, crisp folds often determine the success of a project. Folding paper is a simple technique, but it must be done accurately and precisely for best results.

To obtain clean, sharp folds, you need to carefully measure and score the fold line. Use a bone folder and the grid on your cutting mat to measure and mark your folds. For each fold, draw the bone folder along the ruler edge towards you, pressing down to emboss a fold line. Fold along this embossed line. Use the bone folder to firmly reinforce each fold by smoothing the fold down sharply.

When scoring vellum or parchment, I prefer to use an embossing tool rather than a bone folder. I score the paper lightly and work on a slightly padded surface. If you press too hard when scoring, you can break or split brittle vellum paper.

Fold paper.

Use a bone folder to reinforce the fold after folding.

Gluing

Choosing the appropriate adhesive is important, and so is applying it properly.

Helpful Techniques

- Use a piece of freezer paper to guard your work surface when applying glues.

- For best results, use a piece of card paper like a squeegee to spread a thin layer of glue when working with a thick adhesive. Use a brush for thinner glues.

- Start applying glue in the center of the paper and work the glue to the outside edges. Stroke from the center to the edge to prevent glue buildup at the edges.

- Follow the manufacturer's instructions for using spray adhesive and iron-on fusible adhesive for premium results.

- When gluing paper to a surface, rub the flat edge of a bone folder across the paper for a firm bond. (This is called "rubbing down.") Use a piece of scrap paper when rubbing down to protect the surface of delicate or easily marked papers.

- When adhering a flap to a side of a box with double-sided tape, it is almost impossible to correct a misalignment. Work carefully.

- Too much decoupage finish or white craft glue can cause paper to warp and wrinkle. The glue also can seep under the edges of the paper and destroy the surface.

Gluing Sheets Together

To prevent the formation of wrinkles and bubbles, follow this advice for best results when gluing sheets of paper together.

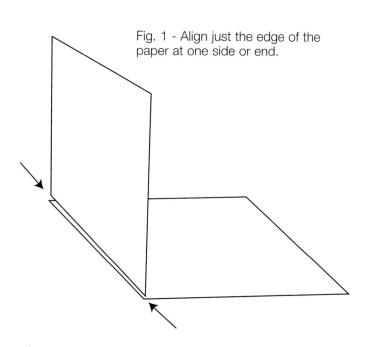

Fig. 1 - Align just the edge of the paper at one side or end.

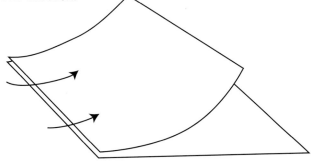

Fig. 2 - Slowly lay the paper down flat, moving in one direction.

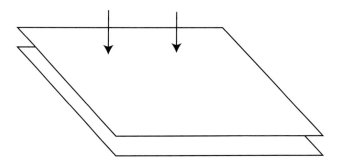

Fig. 3 - Wrong! Don't try to align the paper flat to the surface.

Laminating

Laminating is fusing or gluing lighter-weight papers together to create a stronger material. The technique can also be used to fuse fabric to paper. Adhesives for laminating include fusible iron-on adhesives, spray adhesives, glue sticks, freezer paper, decoupage finish, and adhesive application machines.

Always read the manufacturer's instructions for a perfectly laminated piece, and always laminate materials together before cutting out the package to ensure a good bond on all edges.

With fusible adhesive: This method is good for laminating fabric to paper and paper to paper. Test first, as the adhesive may seep through finer papers. Peel off the protective sheeting and lay the fusible adhesive glue side down on your fabric or paper. Press lightly with an iron. Take off the top protective paper and place the fabric, fusible adhesive glue side down, on the paper. Use the iron on the highest heat setting to press the materials together. Caution: If you iron too much, the adhesive qualities can be lost.

With spray adhesive: Spray the wrong sides of both pieces of paper and place sticky sides together for a good bond. Rub down with a bone folder for a good connection.

With a glue stick: In a pinch or to laminate smaller pieces of paper, together you can use a glue stick. Cover the paper evenly, starting in the center and working to the outside. Place the papers together and rub down firmly.

With freezer paper: You can successfully laminate thin papers, such as fine rice papers and tissue papers, to freezer paper to create a permanently bonded stronger paper. Place the freezer paper, shiny side up, on an ironing board. Place your fine paper on top. With a hot iron, press the materials together. Turn over and press from the other side. Be sure to use a pressing paper between the fine paper and the iron so you do not scorch the fine paper.

This method, when used with fabric, makes a temporary bond that can easily be pulled apart.

With decoupage finish: Use a wide brush to brush the decoupage finish over the paper. When dry, you can press out any wrinkles, using a hot iron with no steam.

With an adhesive application machine: This is by far the simplest, fastest, most effective way to laminate papers together or to apply a plastic laminate coating. Simply place the paper in the machine right side up and turn the crank. This sends the paper through the machine and coats it with an even layer of adhesive. Cut the paper from the machine and peel off the protective backing paper, then align and glue the paper to the card paper or fabric to laminate. If you do not own an adhesive application machine, you can also use adhesive mounting sheets

Decorating Techniques

DECORATIVE PAPERS AVAILABLE FOR PURCHASE ARE VARIED and beautiful, but making your own decorative papers or decorating plain boxes and bags is rewarding and much less expensive. On the following pages, you'll see how to decorate papers and packages. Feel free to combine these techniques to create even more variations.

Sponging

You can create many soft, fascinating patterns with sponging – use acrylic craft paints and a natural sea sponge to decorate card paper or box blanks. You can use just one paint color or a variety of colors. There's no need to completely cover the surface; let color from the background paper show through for interest.

Here's How

1. Dampen the sponge with water and squeeze out the excess.

2. Pour a puddle of paint on a paper plate.

3. Dip the sponge in the paint. Work the paint into the sponge by tapping the sponge on a paper towel. (You don't want too much paint on your sponge or the pattern will be too harsh.)

4. Lightly pounce the sponge on the paper surface with a pouncing motion to create the decorative surface.

Left: Sponging was used to accent the paper that covers this box.

Block Printing

You can buy pre-cut printing blocks or make your own from sponges or spongy materials like computer mouse pads. I like to use waterbase acrylic paint for block printing because it cleans up easily and dries quickly. To print, dip the block in paint or apply paint to the block with a brush or roller, then press to the surface.

- If you want to try making your own blocks, **compressed cellulose sponges** are especially easy to cut. The sponge will expand in thickness when placed in water.

- There are a great many **pre-cut foam blocks** available. All can be used on paper; use the paint and the paint loading technique the manufacturer recommends for best results.

A block printed motif – like this holiday light bulb – can be used to create an overall design on a package with a coordinating gift tag. The motifs are joined by curvy lines that represent the cord. The same motif is used as a tag on a green paper gift bag. The pattern for this design can be found on page 117.

Antiquing Paper

To achieve an antique or old look to your paper, use tea or coffee to stain the paper and give it an ancient patina. I especially like to antique sheets of photocopied labels for use on my packaging projects. Where tea gives a brighter sepia tone, coffee has a soft ivory hue.

Antiquing with a Tea Bag

1. Soak a tea bag in a glass of hot water for 8-10 minutes.

2. Use the tea bag to sponge the strong tea solution onto the paper. Splashes and puddles are okay! Let the paper dry flat.

Antiquing with Coffee

1. Brew strong coffee. (Or use leftover coffee.)

2. With a sponge, apply the coffee to the paper. *Option:* Sprinkle used (damp) coffee grounds on the damp paper for a speckled effect. Let dry flat.

Decoupage

Decoupage is a simple decorative paper treatment that can be used to cover new purchased boxes or ones you are recycling. I like to use torn pieces of decorative papers, fine Japanese papers, and tissue paper that are left over from other projects. I keep a basket full of scraps just for this purpose. Motifs cut out from wrapping paper, paper doilies, pressed flowers and skeleton leaves can also be used to decoupage your project.

You'll Need

1" sponge brush

Decoupage finish

Paper pieces or cutout motifs

Freezer paper (to protect your work surface)

Here's How

1. Cover your work surface with a piece of freezer paper.
2. Brush decoupage finish on the backs of the paper pieces or motifs, working from the center of the paper out to the edges.
3. Arrange the motifs on your surface and use your fingers to smooth out any wrinkles or air bubbles. Overlap the paper pieces or motifs to create interesting compositions. Let dry.
4. Add an additional coat of decoupage finish to protect your finished project.

A recycled cigar box is covered with decorative paper and embellished with postage stamps. The paper was antiqued first then torn into large pieces. The edges of some of the pieces were sponged with a burnt sienna color.

Rubber Stamping

Rubber stamping has become a beautiful art form; it's an easy, elegant way to add images to paper. The range of motifs available in rubber stamps is huge – whatever motif or theme you are looking for, there is a stamp available! Stamps come in tiny sizes that can be repeated for a design and in large sizes for instant coverage. Buy an inkpad with a raised pad so it can be used with any size of stamp.

Rubber Stamping with Ink

Practice on a scrap piece of paper to master the skill of perfect stamping before moving to your project.

Here's How

1. Load the stamp evenly with ink by lightly tapping the stamp on the inkpad.

2. Press the stamp firmly on the surface without rocking the stamp.

Thermal Embossing

Thermal embossing raises the stamped image above the surface of the paper, giving the paper a raised, dimensional surface. There are many embossing powders available – shiny and matte sheens, glitter, iridescents, and metallics – in many different colors.

You'll Need

Paper

Rubber stamp

Pigment inkpad

Embossing powder (the color of your choice)

Embossing heat tool *or* other heat source, such as an iron or toaster oven (Embossing powder melts at 350 degrees F., so a hair dryer will not work.)

Here's How

1. Stamp the image on the paper.

2. While the ink is wet, sprinkle it with embossing powder, completely covering the image.

3. Shake off the excess powder and place back in the jar for later use.

4. *With an embossing tool:* Turn on the embossing heat tool and blow hot air on the stamped image for a few seconds. You will be able to see the powder melt. Do **not** overheat.

With an iron or a toaster oven: Hold the image over the heat source until the powder melts. Be careful not to scorch the paper.

Layered Embossing

This method layers stamped, embossed images and embossing powder to create a pebbly surface with the stamped images. You can experiment with different colors of powders, different stamps, and different colors of inks to create an endless variety of layered embossed surfaces.

You'll Need

A variety of stamps (simple, small motifs work best)

Inkpads with colored ink

Clear embossing powder

Heat embossing tool

Optional: Dense foam sponge

Here's How

1. Choose a stamp. Stamp the image over the surface, using a colored inkpad.

2. While the ink is wet, sprinkle on embossing powder.

3. Shake off excess.

4. Heat the embossing tool and melt the powder.

5. Choose a different motif or a different ink color. Stamp all over the surface and the embossed images.

6. While the ink is wet, sprinkle with embossing powder. Shake off excess.

7. Heat the embossing tools and melt the powder.

8. *Option:* Finish the design by rubbing colored ink on the surface with a dense foam sponge.

The boxes featured below were decorated with stamping (left), and thermal embossing (right).

Faux Leather

This decoupage technique uses crumpled tissue paper to create the look of leather very inexpensively. If you want to make faux leather to cover a box, use a lighter weight paper. You can use a color of tissue paper that suits your project or use paint to color the faux leather.

You'll Need

A sheet of light colored card paper or other paper

A sheet of tissue paper

Decoupage finish

Optional: Acrylic craft paint (color of your choice)

Here's How

1. Crumple the sheet of tissue paper tightly. Release and carefully smooth out the sheet. Set it aside.

2. Brush on a coat of the decoupage finish on the card (or other) paper.

3. Working quickly so the finish does not dry out, place the tissue paper over the wet surface. With your hand, gently smooth the tissue so it bonds with the paper. (The crumpled tissue will create many fine creases and lines that resemble the surface of leather.) Let dry.

4. Brush on a topcoat of decoupage finish to seal and strengthen the paper. Let dry.

5. *Option:* Paint the faux leather with acrylic paint.

A box decorated with the faux leather technique

Gold Leafing

Here's an easy way to add gilded gold-leafed stripes on a project – use double-sided tape. For varying stripe widths, cut strips of tape from a double-sided adhesive sheet with a slide cutter. No covering varnish is needed when working on paper.

You'll Need

Double-sided tape

Gold leaf

Soft brush

Here's How

1. Place the tape where you want the gilded stripe.

2. Remove the backing paper from the tape.

3. Lay gold leaf on the tape.

4. Use a soft brush and gently brush away excess gold leaf, leaving the gilded stripe.

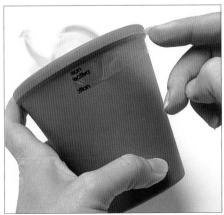

1. Apply tape to the surface.

2. Lay gold leaf on the tape.

3. Use a soft brush to brush away excess.

Using Fabric Paint

Dimensional fabric paints come in squeeze bottles — you can paint with the applicator tip, which makes beads and lines. Typically, these types of paints are permanent, non-toxic, and washable. They come in a wide range of colors and a variety of finishes, including pearls, metallics, glitters, and sparkles. They can be used on paper, fabric, terra cotta, and plastics.

Parchment packages decorated with dimensional fabric paint.

Using Fabric Paint with Glass Beads

This technique can be used on paper, fabric, or plastic. The tiny, holeless glass beads (rather like very tiny marbles) make motifs appear to have been meticulously sewn on – but all you do is sprinkle them on wet fabric paint. (If you are unable to find the tiny glass beads, use the smallest clear seed beads.)

Work in a box (like the top of a shoebox) to catch the excess beads; if you're working on a container, hold the container over a bowl and sprinkle the glass beads on the surface.

You'll Need

Fabric paint with a squeeze applicator

Tiny holeless glass beads (mini marbles), 1 mm-size

Air-erase marker (for fabric)

Surface – fabric *or* a plastic container

Here's How

1. Trace the pattern on fabric with an air-erase marker. If you're using sheer fabric, place the fabric on wax paper with the paper pattern underneath. On a plastic container, you can draw the design freehand or, if the container is clear, place the paper pattern inside the container.
2. Apply fabric paint over the design, tracing the lines carefully.
3. Sprinkle with clear glass beads (marbles). Let dry for 12 hours before using.

A blue plastic bottle was painted with star motifs. Tiny glass beads were pressed in the wet paint.

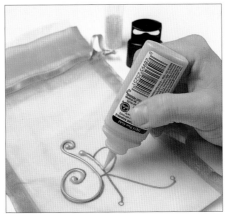

Applying fabric paint to a sheer fabric bag.

Sprinkling the wet paint with tiny glass beads.

Finishing Touches

TAGS, STICKERS, CLIPS, AND EMBELLISHMENTS of all types make your packages distinctive and add your own special touch.

Tags & Labels

Gift tags and cards identify your sentiments and enhance the package. The finest cards and tags are made from the decorative paper used to make the package. Adhere the labels to the card stock with a glue stick or with double-sided tape. Adorn your cards, if you wish, with charms, sayings, or rubber-stamped images. I also like to use copyright-free clip art images – available in books for photocopying or on compact discs for printing on a computer printer – for labels and motifs and for decorating packages.

Use colored felt pens, chalks, or colored pencils to add color and interest to labels. The antiquing technique (with tea or coffee) also works well on labels.

Self-adhesive sticker labels are great for decorative greetings or information, such as a recipe or instructions for use.

Fizzy Bath Salts

Making Your Own Stickers

You can find gorgeous stickers ready to use on your projects or make your own from decorative paper, using double-sided adhesive sheets. Motifs can be cut from the paper used to construct the package for a coordinated designer look.

Here's How

1. Peel away the backing paper on the double-sided adhesive sheet.

2. Apply the sticky side to the wrong side of the paper.

3. Cut out your motif or trim to the size you wish.

4. Peel away the other backing paper and stick in the desired position.

• If the backing paper is difficult to remove, slit 1/2" to the edge with the tip of your scissors for easy lifting.

• If your cutter blade or scissors get gummed up with the sticky film, clean with nail polish remover.

An adhesive application machine makes it easy to apply a thin even coat of adhesive to the back of even the most detailed cut motif or label and instantly make it into a sticker.

Pressed Flower Stickers

Floral stickers can be made ahead and kept until you need to accent a letter, a package, or a card.

Here's How

1. From laminating film, cut a piece large enough to hold the floral arrangement you wish to create.

2. Peel the film from the backing paper and place on your working surface, sticky side up. Arrange the pressed flowers on the sticky film, placing them *right side down*, starting with the largest blossoms, then adding the smaller flowers and filler pieces and, finally, the greenery. Remember you are building your design from front to back. If you don't press down the flowers, it may be possible to move them around a bit. This is not recommended, however, as the flowers are very fragile and will most likely fall apart.

3. When you are pleased with the arrangement, check it by picking up the laminating paper and taking a peek underneath. Place it on another piece of laminating film.

4. Cut out the arrangement no closer than 1/8" to the flowers.

5. To use, peel away the remaining backing paper and place on your project.

Tag & Label Designs

Photo copy these images to use on your labels and gift tags.

Making Wire Clips

It is easy to form wire into your own decorative wire fasteners. Most designs use 18 gauge colored copper wire (it's easy to find in craft stores). You can also use soft aluminum 3/16" armature wire to make oversized wire closures. Areas of the wire, such as the center of a daisy, can be colored with embossing powder.

Here's How

1. Using one of the patterns on page 117 or one you draw yourself, coil and form the wire with needlenose pliers. Use wire cutters to trim and cut the wire. *Option:* Use a clear peg-type jig: Place the clear jig over the pattern, align the pegs with the turns in the design, and form the pieces with the wire. (This method is very useful when making more than one of a design.)

2. Flatten the formed wire piece with a hammer on a hard, flat surface. (Flattened pieces are stronger and hold the paper together better.)

3. Adjust the pieces as needed to their original forms after hammering.

To color:

1. Sponge rubber stamp pigment ink on a section of the flattened wire clip with a dense foam sponge.

2. Sprinkle with clear or colored embossing powder and melt the powder. Let the wire cool before touching it – it is very hot. Handle carefully and use only on small areas, as the colored plastic coating can rub off or chip.

Patterns can be found on page 117.

Using Polymer Clay

Stamped Polymer Clay

You can create beautiful seals and embellishments with polymer clay, rubber stamps, and metallic powders.

Here's How

1. Roll a small amount of clay in a small ball. Flatten slightly.

2. Push a rubber stamp in the clay to create a decorative impression.

3. With your finger, rub on metallic powder to accent the stamped design.

4. Bake the clay in your home oven, following the manufacturer's instructions.

- **For larger embellishments,** such as the label on this clay pot, roll out a small, thin sheet of polymer clay. Press your stamp in the soft clay. Cut out the shape, position on the clay pot, and bake right on the pot. After the clay is baked, it can be sanded, sealed with waterbase varnish, and painted to bring out the details. Glue the label to the pot with white craft glue.

- **For the leaf tag,** find a fresh leaf that is strong and has a detailed vein pattern on the underside. (Rose, camellia, sweet bay, and apple leaves all work well.) Form a small piece of clay into a rough leaf shape and press into the underside of the leaf to get an impression of the veins. Place the clay leaf on a piece of aluminum foil and press a motif or letters in

the soft clay with rubber stamps, pressing so the design is deeply impressed but not so hard that you push through to the bottom. With a sharp point (a skewer or a toothpick), make a hole in the top of the leaf. Bake according to the manufacturer's instructions. After the clay is baked, it can be sanded, sealed with waterbase varnish, and painted to bring out the details.

Raffia-Winged Bee Tag

*These stamped, winged bees can be cut out and adhered to a clothespin for a quick parcel closure **or** glued directly to a card or parcel as an embellishment.*

Here's How

1. Cut the bee body from compressed sponge using the pattern supplied. Use an art knife to cut out the stripe details.

2. Place the sponge in water to make it expand. Squeeze out excess moisture.

3. Place the sponge into a puddle of black acrylic paint. Press the bee stamp on yellow paper. Let dry completely.

4. Cut out the bee shape.

5. Take a 12" piece of raffia and form a four-loop bow for the bee's wings.

6. Tie a 6" piece of raffia in the middle of the bow to hold it in shape and to form the bee's antennae.

7. Glue the raffia wings in place on the back of the stamped bee with a glue gun.

Pattern for Bee

Making Colored Brads

Paper brads are found in a variety of sizes in stationery stores and office supply outlets. You can find colored or fancy topped brads in scrapbooking and rubber stamp stores or you can color ordinary gold brads using the following technique.

Here's How

1. Hold the brad with needlenose pliers. (You **must** hold the brad with the pliers – if you don't, you'll burn your fingers.) Press the flat top on a pigment stamp pad in the color of your choice, then dip the top of the brad in clear embossing powder.

2. With the embossing heat tool, melt the embossing powder to seal the color. **Caution:** The brad is very hot! Let it cool completely before touching the top.

How to Cover a Box

HERE'S AN EASY WAY to cover just about any box with decorative paper. After trying many methods that involved complicated measuring, cutting multiple pieces, and dealing with unsightly seams, I came up with this simple procedure you see on the following pages.

Pictured clockwise from top:

The **Letter Box** is a recycled box. The top was covered with an antiqued script-patterned decorative paper. A gilded stripe, a punched label, and a polymer clay seal were added to decorate.

The **Photo Box** is a purchased papier mache box. The top was covered with handmade paper and the bottom with botanical wrapping paper. A contrasting burgundy suede paper was used to line the top and bottom. Motifs cut from the wrapping paper, contrasting handmade paper, and stickers were used to enhance the box top.

The **Pear Box** is a recycled box that was covered with matching decorative papers and decorated with a matching sticker, a gift card, and a gold sheer ribbon bow.

The **Botanical Box** is a papier mache box covered with decoupage paper and handmade paper. The flaps formed on the long sides of the box form an interesting added detail. The edges of the flap and the top and bottom box edges were sponged with gold acrylic paint to accent. Brads were added to the long ends.

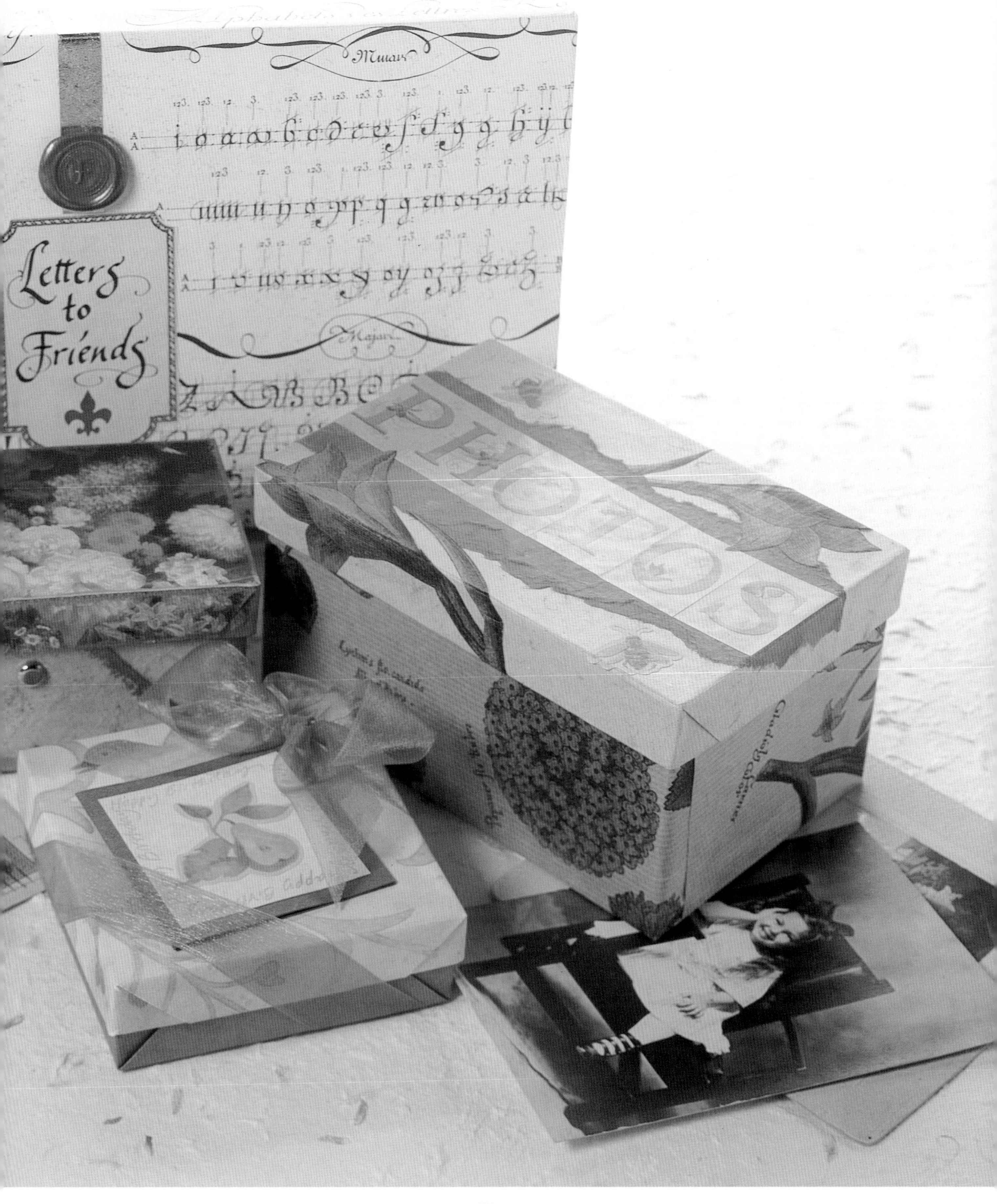
Letters to Friends
PHOTOS

Steps to Cover a Box

This method uses two pieces of paper (one for the box base and one for the lid) and covers the outside and the sides of the inside. (You can cut panels to line the inside of the lid and box bottom.) Use a glue stick to adhere the paper. You also can use decoupage finish as a glue and give the box a few coats of decoupage finish to seal. Apply the adhesive as you work, making sure every piece is glued down, and use the bone folder, rubbing down firmly and into the corners to ensure a clean job.

1. **Measure and cut paper**
   - To start, cut a piece of decorative paper to cover the box. Lighter weight paper is easier to handle than heavier weight paper. Handmade papers or wrapping papers are good choices for covering; suede paper can be used to line the inside of the lid and the inside bottom of the base.
   - To calculate the size of paper, follow this formula:
   (Height x 4) + (length) by (height x 4) + (width) = size

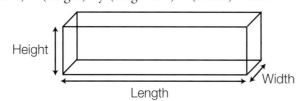

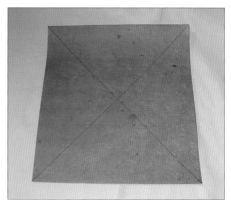

Photo 1

   - As an example, let's cover a box whose base is 1-1/2" high, 3-3/4" long, and 1-3/4" wide. Using the formula above, here's how to calculate the size of the paper needed:
   (1-1/2" x 4") + 3-3/4" by (1-1/2" x 4") + 1-3/4" = 9-3/4" by 7-3/4"
   - Since I always add a bit to make sure the side pieces overlap slightly on the inside bottom of the box, I'd use a piece of paper 10" x 8".
   - Next, cut the paper panels for the inside bottom of the base and the inside of the lid. Measure the box carefully and cut the pieces 1/8" smaller than the dimensions so the panels fit snugly.

2. With an air erase pen, make two lines, corner to corner, so you can position the box in the exact center of the paper. *See photo 1.*

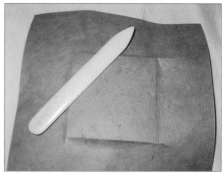

Photo 2

3. Apply a thin layer of adhesive on the wrong side of the decorative paper in the middle section. Position the box in the center of the paper and turn over. Rub down the paper to adhere to the bottom of the box with the bone folder to bond and prevent wrinkles. Run the side of the bone folder along the paper down the edges of the box. (This helps prevent pockets from forming along this edge after the paper is folded over.) *See photo 2.*

4. Turn the box over. Apply the adhesive to one of the long sides of the paper and fold up. With scissors, cut straight down to the top of the box at both corners as indicated. Continue to wrap the paper and adhere it to the inside of the box. Use a ruler on larger boxes and mark the cutting line to ensure a clean, straight cut. Repeat on the other side of the box. *See photo 3.*

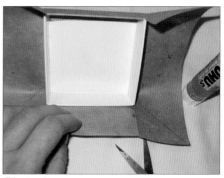

Photo 3

5. Fold in the paper on the two remaining ends snug into the box. You will form pointed ends, much like wrapping a gift box. It is easier to make the folds first. Rub down firmly with the bone folder, then undo the folds and apply the glue. *See photo 4.*

6. Glue the remaining sides and points into the sides and into the inside of the box, rubbing down firmly. *Variation:* Adhere the points to the underside of the box. *See photo 5.*

7. With the bone folder, press down all sides and inside corners to make sure the paper is adhered well. *See photo 6.*

8. Glue the panels inside the lid and inside the bottom of the base. *Option:* Cut a panel for the outside bottom of the box 1/4" smaller than the dimensions of the box bottom. *See photo 7.*

Photo 4

Photo 5

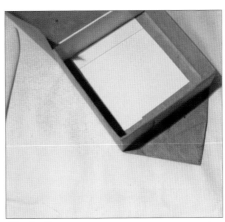
Photo 6

Photo 7

TIPS

• If you're using a recycled box, be sure any printing on the box does not show through the paper. If it does, spray paint or brush on a coat of white primer to mask the printing before covering the box.

• For boxes with steep sides, you may need to adjust the paper size slightly for the end points to fold neatly. I cut the paper according to the formula; as I work, I adjust the size by cutting as needed.

Covering a Box with Fabric

You can also cover a box with fabric, using the same technique and adhesives you'd use for paper.

Making Gift Boxes

USING THE PATTERNS IN THIS BOOK to make your own templates for boxes gives you the freedom to use the paper of your choice and to adjust the pattern for variations. I have included a variety of box patterns. They are all easy to put together and fun to decorate.

When you make boxes, be sure all the edges are straight and the box sides are square. The more care you take, the fewer the problems you will have making boxes. **Patterns for box shapes can be found on pages 118-126**

TIPS

• When constructing a new box shape, test the design with an inexpensive paper to make sure you have the dimensions and size right before you use your decorative paper.

• When choosing a paper for making a box or package, consider what you are placing in it. Generally, you can use lighter papers for smaller boxes, and you'll need heavier card weight paper for larger boxes. Heavier objects require a sturdier package.

• Consider variations, such as changing the size and dimensions to create a different size and look, adding a window, or changing the closure method.

• To make a new parcel template, find a box or package you like, take it apart, and use it as your pattern.

Templates

Templates are the shapes you trace around to make packages. They are made of a traced pattern laminated to card paper and can be used again and again.

Making Templates for Packages

You'll Need:

Pattern for the package

Tracing paper

Pencil

Laminating paper

Cutting mat

Ruler

Art knife

Here's How

1. Trace the pattern from this book carefully on tracing paper. Make the cutting lines solid and the scoring lines dotted. (Like they are on the pattern.) Adjust the size if you wish by enlarging or reducing the traced design on a photocopier.

2. On the tracing (or photocopy), write any information you wish to remember that will help in the construction of the box, such as the finished size of the box or the panel in which to add a window.

3. Laminate the paper pattern to a piece of card paper. For a stronger template, laminate the top of the pattern with a plastic sheet.

4. Cut out your template, using a cutting mat, ruler, and art knife for a straight-edged template. (Scissors will not give you the precise edges you need for successful boxes.)

5. *Option:* Cut out small triangles to mark score lines. (This will enable you to mark the paper easily.)

Constructing a Package with a Template

You'll Need

Template

Air-erase pen *or* a pencil

Glue stick *or* double-sided tape (for gluing lighter seams and labels)

White craft glue *or* glue gun and glue sticks (for heavier seams and embellishments)

Art knife

Cutting mat

Ruler

Scissors

Bone folder

Paper (cover stock or laminated papers)

Here's How

1. Use a little piece of low-tack tape to tape the template to the paper.

2. Trace the outside of the package with an air-erase pen.

3. Leaving the template in place, mark the scoring lines by making little marks on the paper outside of the template.

4. Remove the template. Score where indicated, lining up the marks on the paper with your straight edge. You can 'over draw' these lines to the outside of the traced lines to make the score lines fold easier.

5. Cut out the package shape along the solid lines.

6. Fold and rub down the scored lines.

7. Glue the flaps to form the package. *Tip:* It is generally best to glue down the longer edges first.

8. Decorate your finished box.

Quick Box

The quick box is a very simple, template-free, fast technique for making a lidded box. Standard card weight paper can be used for making any box up to 4" x 6". For larger boxes, a heavier card paper or card paper laminated with decorative paper should be used. You could also choose a decorative, lighter card paper for the box top and a heavier card paper for the bottom.

To make the box, you will need two pieces of paper, both cut to the same size. You can use any size rectangle or square for your box.

PAPER SIZE GUIDE

Paper Size	*Finished Box Size (width x length x height)*
2" x 3"	1" x 1-1/2" x 1/2"
3" x 4"	1-1/2" x 2" x 3/4"
4" x 5"	2" x 2-1/2" x 1"
5" x 6"	2-1/2" x 3" x 1-1/4"
6" x 7"	3" x 3-1/2" x 1-1/2"
7" x 8"	3-1/2" x 4" x 1-3/4"

Here's How

1. On your pieces of paper, draw a diagonal line from the top left corner to bottom right corner with an air-erase marker. Repeat with the opposite corners to form an X. Repeat on the second piece of paper. (Fig. 1)

2. On the piece of paper that will be your box top, make a 1/4" circle at the intersection of the X. (Fig. 2) *Tip:* Make a simple template by punching a 1/4" hole in a piece of plastic and use it for making your quick boxes. (The circle size is always the same, regardless of the size of the box.)

3. Fold the long sides of the box bottom piece to the exact center of the X. Unfold. Fold the shorter sides to the middle of the X. (Fig. 3)

4. Fold the long sides of the box top piece to the outside of the circle. Unfold. Fold the shorter sides to the outside of the circle. (This makes the box top slightly larger than the box bottom for a perfect fit.)

Fig. 1 - Box bottom

Fig. 2 - Box top

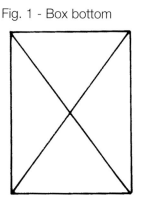

Fig. 3

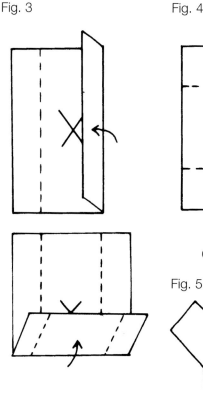

Fig. 4

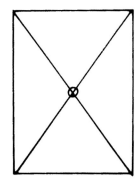

Cut   Cut

Fig. 5

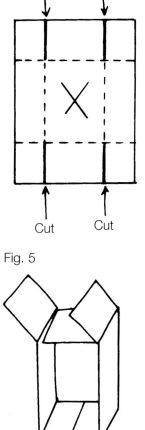

← Trim

5. Cut four slits on the shorter sides on both the top and bottom pieces. This makes the flaps and the ends. (Fig. 4)

6. Bring the flap ends together at right angles to the whole piece, forming the sides of the box. (Fig. 5) Fold in or trim off the excess at the top. Repeat on the other side.

7. Using a glue stick or double-sided tape, adhere the flaps to form the box lid and the box bottom.

Pictured Top: The top of this quick box was made of an enlarged photocopy of a photograph laminated to card paper. The bottom was made of plain card paper.

Pictured Bottom: This example is a variation of the quick box. I made only a box bottom. The top is a piece of corrugated cardboard cut to the width of the box bottom and glued to the bottom. It wraps up and around, forming the lid. The lid is held closed by a piece of twine glued on the bottom of the box. It is brought up through an eyelet and tied in a bow. The box is decorated with rubber stamped paper and accented with coiled wire, a bee charm, and a silk leaf.

Square Box

The square box and its lid are folded from one cut piece. (You can also purchase this box as a blank or a stencil template.) To make one using the pattern, follow the instructions elsewhere in this book for making a template, cutting, and scoring. To assemble, fold in and glue the side tabs.

Pattern can be found on page 118.

Pictured above left and right: The panorama boxes are assembled with a small square box of colored card paper inside a larger box made from clear plastic sheet. The smaller paper box, which holds the gift, is placed in the larger clear box and small items are placed between the two boxes. Sand and shells were added for the **Beach Scene Box**, which has a raffia bow. Polyester fiberfill, mini pom-poms, and snowflake sequins fill the space inside the **Snow Scene Box**, which is wrapped with white rickrack.

Pictured opposite page: These square lidded boxes were constructed from flat box blanks. On the small green box, I added a ribbon lid-pull that is threaded through an eyelet in the lid. The small crackled-look box is decorated with a Chinese coin, cording, and beads. The small flower motif box is rubber stamped. Brads accent the flower centers. The bottom of the large box was rubber-stamped and embossed; the top was adorned with beaded berries, velvet leaves, a gold mesh ribbon bow, and a brass bee charm.

Pictured above: The **Button Top Box**, is made from a lidded box blank that was covered with paper. It is held closed with elastic cording and decorated with a big red button.

Origami Box

Folded origami boxes are designed to be made from lighter papers. They are quick and easy to construct; you can stack them or present many boxes nested together. The decorative paper shows on the inside and the outside of the box.

Here's How

1. Cut two pieces of paper, one 6" square for the bottom and the other 6-3/16" square for the top. This will make a 2" square box that is 1" high.

Fig. 1

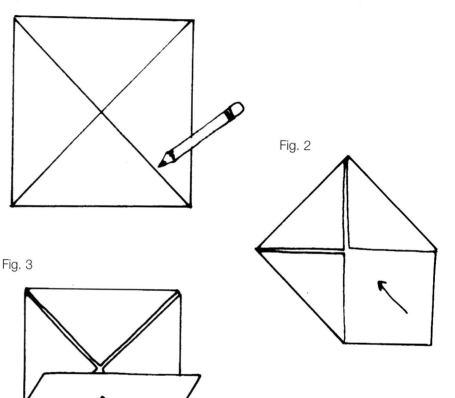

Fig. 2

Fig. 3

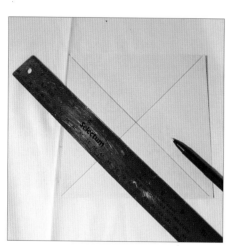

2. Mark an X from corner to corner with an air-erase marker on the wrong sides of the paper.

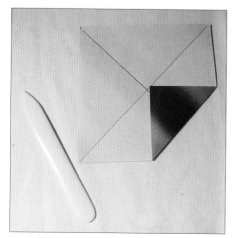

3. Fold in a corner to the center of the square. Use a bone folder to crease the folds for a hard edge.

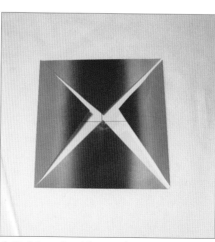

4. Fold each side to the center mark and crease. (Fig. 2)

5. Unfold. Repeat with the remaining sides. (Fig. 3) Cut as indicated.

Continued on page 58

The love of flowers
is really the best teacher
of how to grow and
understand them.
~ Max Schling

Continued from page 56

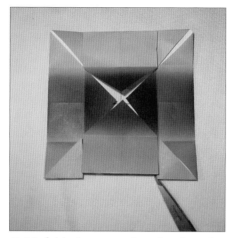

Fig. 4

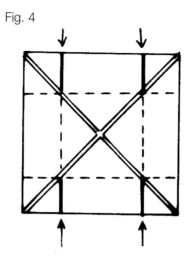

Fig. 5

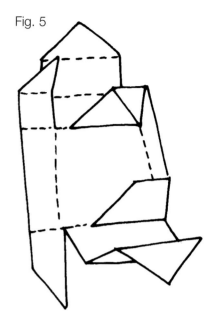

6. Unfold the cut edge, leaving the remaining sides folded to form two opposite walls of the box. (Fig. 4)

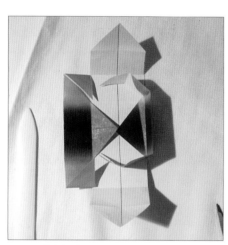

Fig. 6

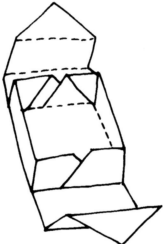

Fig. 7

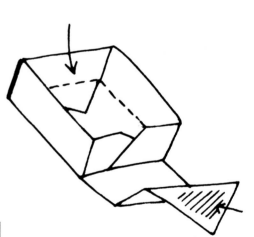

7. Unfold the corners of the other sides and fold the pointed sides up and over. (Fig. 5 & 6)

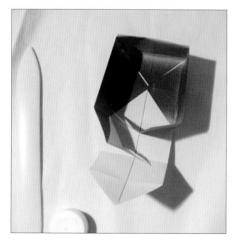

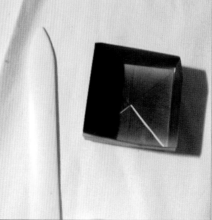

8. Add a small bit of glue to the pointed ends and glue to the bottom of the box to secure. (Fig. 7)

Finished Box

Pictured on opposite page: A stack of origami boxes in graduated sizes

Collapsible Box

The collapsible box is wonderful for holding flat items – the box collapses around the gift, enclosing it. It is held closed with a strip of paper or ribbon. To open the box, slip off the band and pull the pointed flaps. The box will pop open to reveal the contents.

To make a contrasting lining for your box, fuse two pieces of decorative paper with spray adhesive. Do not make the fused papers too thick or the box will be difficult to fold.

You'll Need (for one box, 4" square)

2 pieces decorative paper (see Fig. 1)

Strip of decorative paper, 10" x 3/4"
or a piece of ribbon, 10" long

Spray adhesive

Ruler

Art knife

Glue

Here's How

1. Measure and cut out 2" squares from the corners of the fused together sheet. (Fig. 1)

2. Measure and score all the dotted lines as shown (Fig. 1) for easy folding. Measure carefully and precisely.

3. Fold and crease along all scored lines, then open the paper piece out flat with the inside of the box facing down.

continued on page 62

Fig. 1a
Cutting & Folding Diagram for a 4" Collapsible Box
Paper Size: 8" x 12"

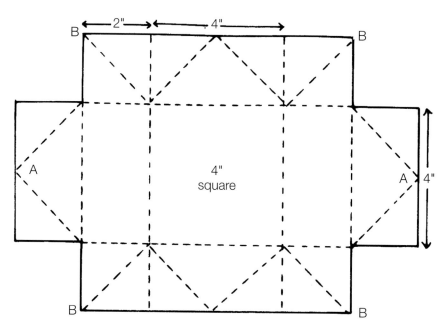

Fig. 1b
Cutting & Folding Diagram for a 3-1/2" Collapsible Box
Paper size: 10-5/8" x 7"

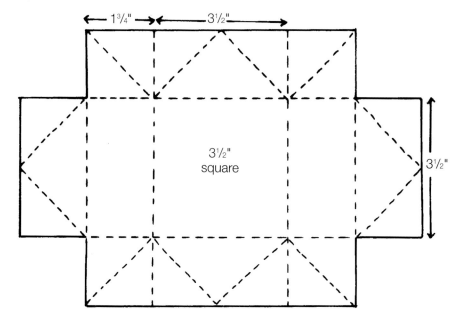

continued from page 60

4. Fold each corner on flap A to form an arrow. (Fig. 2) Glue to hold.

5. Turn over so the inside faces up. Pinch the B corners outward to bring the sides up. (Fig. 3) Tuck and glue the pointed corner to the side. (You will now have a box.)

6. With your fingers, push in and collapse the top and bottom sides, pressing the box flat. Crease well. (Fig. 4)

7. Make the band by wrapping the paper strip or ribbon around the box. Glue where the paper or ribbon ends overlap.

Fig. 1c
Cutting & Folding Diagram for a 3" Collapsible Box
Paper size: 9" x 6"

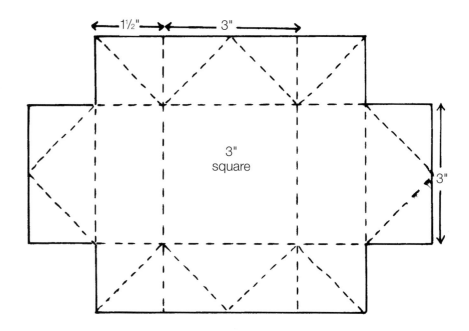

Fig. 2

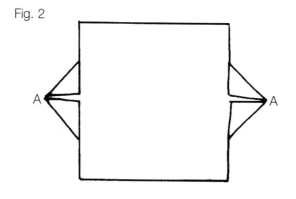

Fig. 3

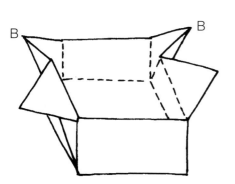

Fig. 4

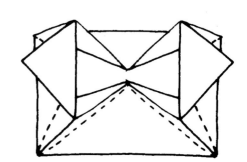

Match Box

These pretty little boxes are made with a stencil template. You can get the same look by making a small rectangular quick box for the base and wrapping a piece of card paper around it.

The blue match box, *above*, was constructed from blue card paper and decorated with a sticker border, a label, and a plastic button. (I removed the shank from the button before gluing it on the box.) Covering the other match box with decorative script-motif paper makes for an elegant look. Ribbon and a polymer clay seal are used as accents. It's perfect for holding stamps on your desk.

Shaped Boxes

Here's a very quick and easy way to make shaped boxes. I liked the idea of creating shaped boxes, but the techniques I tried were complicated and time consuming. When I discovered the die-cut machines at scrapbooking and rubber stamp stores could cut mat board, I had found the answer to my quandary of making quick and easy shaped boxes.

You'll Need (for one box)

2 identical shapes cut from mat board (see ideas below)

Acrylic craft paint

Glue gun *or* white craft glue

Paper (to make a Quick Box or Origami Box) or a small box

Here's How

1. Paint the shapes with acrylic paint on all sides. Let dry.

2. Construct a quick box or an origami box to fit between the shapes.

3. Glue the bottom of the box to one shape.

4. Place the top of the box on the bottom. Place the top shape on the top of the box and align perfectly with the bottom shape.

5. Glue the shape to the top of the box.

6. Decorate as you like.

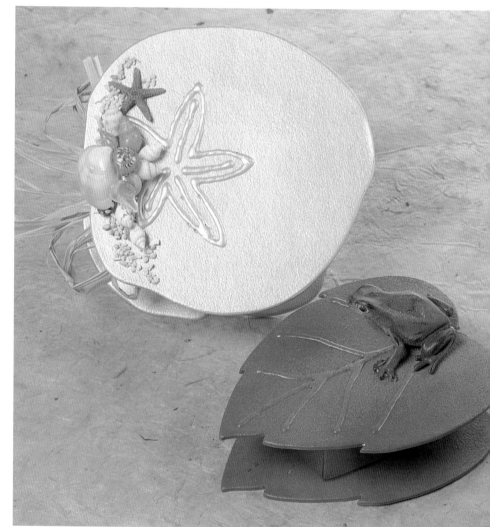

Here are some sample ideas for shaped boxes:

Pictured Top: The **Sand Dollar Box** starts with sand dollar shapes and a 2-1/2" square quick box. Details on the top sand dollar were highlighted with fabric paint before painting with champagne colored paint. Shells, sand, and a gold seahorse charm were glued to the top. A raffia bow was added to the underside of the top shape.

Pictured Bottom: The veins on the top leaf of the **Frog Box** were accented with fabric paint to raise the details before painting with green acrylic paint. The plastic frog was sponged with pigment stamp ink and embossed with pearl green embossing powder for a metallic, fancy look.

Pictured clockwise from top:

The shapes for the **Jingle Bell Box** came in two parts and were painted separately with metallic paints. Circles were cut from red card paper and glued under both painted shapes to reinforce them before they were glued to a red box. Silk greenery, berries, and a gold cord finish off this seasonal box.

The romantic **Scalloped Heart Box** has a decoupaged motif on top and silver details made with fabric paint. A rose charm and a thread tassel were added as accents.

Simple 3" squares cut from black mat board were used to make the **Graduation Hat Box**. I made a hole in the middle of the top board and added a gold brad and tassel before gluing it to the top of the box.

Pyramid Boxes

Pyramid boxes are made from one piece. Follow the instructions in this book for making a template (page 51), cutting (page 24), and scoring (page 25). Fold in and glue the side tabs. You can choose to glue three sides together and leave one to open or to not glue any tabs and have the box able to open out flat. The pyramid box is another shape that can be found as a flat box blank, ready to rubber stamp, sponge, or decorate.

Pattern can be found on page 119.

Open pyramid boxes, pictured clockwise from top left: Stacked Black Box, Asian-inspired Box, Sponged Blue Box

Pictured on opposite page, clockwise from top:

- The **Stacked Black Box** is two boxes glued together – a black pyramid box on a black lidded square box. Before gluing, a gilded gold leafed strip was added on each side of the pyramid box, square box lid, and square box base. Two loops were attached to the square box bottom and brought up and over the pyramid box top to hold. The top was adorned with copper wire and beads that – when the pyramid box is opened – holds a hanging ornament.

- The **Sponged Blue Box** has a top lid created by cutting off the box top before gluing the flaps together. The lid and base were accented with copper tape. Fibers and beads were added as embellishments.

- The **Rubber Stamped Pyramid** is held together with two loops of gold elastic cord that were glued to the box base and covered with a panel. The cords are looped over the top point to hold the box together.

- The **Sandpaper Pyramid** has a suede panel glued to the bottom so the box will not scratch the table surface. It was adorned with fibers and beads and a polymer clay seal. The closure is a black cord threaded through holes at the top of the box and tied together.

- The **Asian-inspired Box** holds a smaller pyramid box inside. The closure is a square piece of heavy card laminated with decorative paper. A small square is cut from the middle and placed on the box to hold it together.

Cornucopia Box

The cornucopia box is a four-sided cone shape that can be left plain or decorated in a variety of ways. From small to large, these boxes are easy to make and also are available in flat box blanks.

The box is made all in one piece and has a flap-type lid. Follow the instructions elsewhere in this book for making a template (page 51), cutting (page 24), and scoring (page 25), then fold in and glue the side tabs.

Pattern can be found on page 120

Pictured at left, counter-clockwise from top:

The two satin-and-lace-covered boxes have different top treatments. The satin was fused to the card paper before the box template was cut out. Lace motifs and pearls cover the seams and ribbon flowers have been added as accents.

- **Pincushion Box** has a pincushion on top that was constructed from a circle of matching fabric. It was sewn, gathered, and stuffed with polyester fiberfill, then glued to the box lid. A piece of thin ribbon, glued under the pincushion, is used as a closure – the ribbon is held down (and the box held closed) with a hook-and-loop fastener dot hidden under the lace posy.

- **Lace Pouch Box** – the top and flaps were cut off and a lace pouch was glued in. A string of pearls accents the top edge and hides the cut edges.

- The **Lace Top Box** has a sheer white bag glued in the box. A silver charm with a rhinestone and silver tassels accents the front.

Continued on page 70

Pictured on the previous page:
The interesting natural papers used to make two of the cornucopias at left were rubber-stamped and laminated on card paper before the boxes were cut out. Raffia, ribbon, a seal, and a button were used for finishing accents.

• The **Amor Cornucopia** is trimmed with gold braid and a gold-rubbed polymer clay seal.

• **Raffia-trimmed Cornucopia**, the box lid flaps on the box were enlarged before cutting, then brought to the middle to create a different box top. An African-theme button, its shank removed, was glued to one side.

• **Clear Cornucopia Box** is wonderful for showing off the contents. This little box holds mulling spices and is dressed up with a gold ribbon, a red seal, and whole spices glued to the lid.

Pictured at right, counter-clockwise from top:
• **Large Floral Cornucopia Box** was created with embossed decorative paper. A three-dimensional decoupage motif was cut from the same paper, brushed with clear varnish to make it sturdier, and glued to the front using silicone glue.

• **Embossed Vellum Cornucopia Box**, which is slightly smaller, was made from matching embossed vellum paper. Coordinating stickers were used to decorate it, and a ribbon loop in the center of the lid allows the box to be displayed by hanging.

• **Flower-topped Box** can be quickly decorated for a wedding to hold petals for strewing, candy favors, birdseed, or a piece of wedding cake. It's available as flat box blank from wedding supply stores. The flowers and leaves were punched out of vellum and adhered to the constructed box with a glue gun. The beaded-look center and hearts were added with fabric paint. A thin satin bow is a finishing touch.

• **Parchment Cornucopia** has eyelets that were added to the sides before construction. A wire handle, hooked into the reinforced holes, can be used to hang or carry the box. A pressed flower sticker holds down a thin ribbon tie that completes the design.

Pillow Pouch

Pillow pouches are available as flat box blanks, stencil templates, and ready-made boxes in a variety of sizes, and you can make them yourself. The box is made in one piece with ends that lift open. Follow the instructions in this book for making a template (page 51), cutting (page 24), and scoring (page 25), but use the edge of a plate to score the curved fold lines. The tab with the notch is folded in first so the pouch is easily opened. Windows can be easily added to the front panel before constructing the pouch. The simple design allows you to give the pillow pouch a variety of looks.

Pattern can be found on page 121.

Pictured this page, top to bottom:

- **Large Cookie Pouch**, made from corrugated cardboard, is strong enough to hold a batch of home-made cookies. Place the cookies in a cellophane or waxed bag before placing them in the pouch. Decorations include vintage-look stickers, a raffia bow, a button, and miniature clothespins.

- **Clear Pouches** are easy to make from clear plastic sheets. The flaps are glued down with double-sided tape. The pouches are filled with botanical potpourri, which is decorative and fragrant. They are not meant to be opened.

- **Photo Pouch** is cut from an enlarged photocopy of a photograph that was laminated on card paper. A gold elastic cord, placed diagonally, holds the gift tag.

Pictured on the opposite page, clockwise from top:

- **Window Pouch,** this rust-colored pouch has an oval window covered with patterned vellum paper. Fibers and cords are adorned with beads and tied around the pouch. The gift tag is a preserved leaf. The greeting was written with a gold paint pen.

- **Ivory Pouch** is an elegant pouch made from embossed decorative paper. It's accented with sheer ribbon, a gold bouillon wire bow, and a gold charm.

• For the trio of nature-inspired pouches, decorative paper was fused to heavier card paper. The **Bee Pouch** and **Dragonfly Pouch** have windows covered with brass mesh. The butterfly on the **Butterfly Pouch** and the dragonfly on the Dragonfly Pouch were made from stickers that were stuck on card paper and cut out. Curled wire antennae were added.

Pointed Paper Pouch

These cute pouches are perfect for small gifts. The front pocket can hold a card, a candy cane, or another little goodie.

Pictured above:

The pocket on the **Christmas Pouch** holds a candy cane. It's trimmed with gold metallic rick-rack. A red button is laced with gold cording that holds the top closure in place.

Instructions follow on page 76.

Pictured above:
Larger and smaller pointed paper pouches can be made from a variety of papers. The top of a smaller pouch can be folded over and held with a swirl clip. Or close the small pouch with a brad that also holds a tag.

continued from page 74

Fig. 1

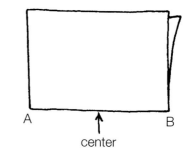

You'll Need (for one larger pouch)

1 sheet of decorative or handmade paper, 8-1/2" x 11"

Strip of card paper, 5" x 2-1/2"

Two - 8 1/2" x 5 1/2" (1/2 sheet) handmade paper or glassine paper

Here's How

1. Fold the decorative paper in half width-wise, with the right side of the paper on the inside. (Fig. 1)

2. Fold corners A and B to the center diagonally. Crease the folds firmly. (Fig. 2)

3. Fold corners C and D to the center. Crease the folds. (Fig. 3)

4. Fold the top flaps to the inside and glue to hold. (Fig. 4)

5. Fold the card paper strip in half lengthwise and place over top of pouch. Punch two holes in the top through all the layers.

6. Use a twig or a ribbon to hold large pouches together.

Fig. 2

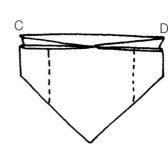

Fig.3

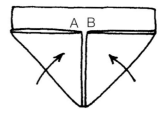

Fig. 4

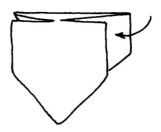

Interlocking Box

Two flaps on the top and bottom of this lidded box are oversized to form a clever interlocking assembly. The bottom and top are cut from the same pattern and assembled the same way. Different colors and types of paper can be used for an attractive contrast.

Pattern can be found on page 122

Here's How

1. Follow the instructions elsewhere in this book for making a template, cutting, and scoring.

2. Fold in and glue the side tabs to the inside of each long side. When interlocking the top and bottom, tuck the long sides to the inside of the box.

3. Push the two pieces together gently with all four flaps on the inside, to close the box.

Pictured at right:
The **Tall Interlocking Box** has a bottom deeper than the top for a different-shaped package. When adjusting the pattern, make the middle square the same for both the top and the bottom. For the bottom, add the same amount to all four sides. It's accented with a sticker label, letters, and a polymer clay seal.

The top and bottom of the **Square Interlocking Box** were made from the same pattern. The top was made from a piece of embossed vellum and the bottom from matching card paper. A gold-edged label, bee stickers, and a polymer clay seal accent the finished box.

Paper Purse

These whimsical little purses are fun containers for favors or small gifts. The basic pattern can be adjusted to create many different looks, sizes, and closure designs. The purse is done with one piece. Follow the instructions in the Basic Techniques section for cutting and scoring, then fold in and glue the side tabs to the insides of the front and back.

Patterns can be found on page 123

Pictured at right, clockwise from top:

- **Posy-topped Purse** has a solid, rounded top. It was cut from vellum paper that had been fused to lightweight white paper. A punched posy with punched leaves has a brass brad center that holds the purse closed.

- **Autumn Leaf Purse** was made with natural paper laminated to card paper. The rounded top flap covers a hook-and-loop dot that keeps the purse closed. Leaf stickers and a metal button finish the design.

- **Suede Paper Purse** sports a color-coordinated cord handle and a silk flower accent on the flap. A hook-and-loop dot provides closure.

- **Asian Coin Purse** was cut from Japanese paper laminated to card paper. The coin and tassel decorate the purse; a hook-and-loop dot holds it closed.

Column Twist Container

Column twist containers are easy and quick to make. No template is necessary, and you can adjust the paper size to create different size and shape variations. Hold the top closed with a wire clip, decorative sticker, or brad.

Pictured above, left to right:

• **Seashore Container** is made from a sheet of sandpaper. It is filled with vermiculite (found at garden supply stores) that has been infused with fragrance oils. This charming scented sachet is decorated with shells, pebbles, and a lighthouse. It can be displayed but is not meant to be opened.

• **Topiary Container**, trimmed with artificial rose hips and raffia, is made from a plain paper and decorated with stickers.

• **Butterfly Container** is decorated with a butterfly gift tag with wire antennae. It is closed with a brass brad.

• The **Bird & Fruit Container** is made from rust-colored paper and decorated with a variety of stickers. Sticker borders – instead of paper strips – were used to trim the top and bottom of the container.

Instructions follow on next page.

continued from page 79

Fig. 1 Fig. 2 Fig. 3

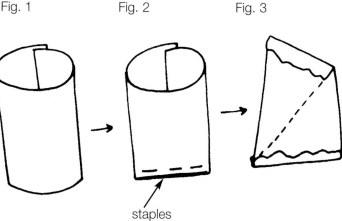

staples

Here's How

1. Start with a rectangular piece of paper. (Many times I use paper pieces left over from other packages.) Place a piece of double-sided tape along one edge of the panel and roll the panel into a cylinder. (Fig. 1) Rub down the seam so it adheres well.

2. Pinch one end (the bottom) of the cylinder together and staple to hold. (Fig. 2)

3. Pinch the other end (the top) of the cylinder at right angles to the bottom to form the package. (Fig. 3)

4. Cut a strip of matching paper, score it down the center, and glue it over the bottom of the pouch to hide the staples.

5. Cut two paper strips and glue them to the top of the cylinder, leaving the top open so you can insert the gift.

Pictured opposite:
The three **Nursery Rhyme Containers** are made of decorative paper in soft coordinating hues. The paper strips on the tops and bottoms of the pouches are cut with decorative-edge scissors. Swirl wire clips hold the tops closed.

Pictured on this page, clockwise from top left:
This trio shows the variety of papers that can be used for this container.

- The **Cardboard Container** is made from lightweight corrugated cardboard. A large button is attached with gold cording and the package is held closed with a gold cord loop.

- The **Leaf Container** is made from fused vellum. A copper wire clip holds a gift tag made from a skeleton leaf.

- The **Swirl Container,** with metallic swirl motifs are echoed in the closure – a silver metal swirl clip.

Triangle Long Box

Large or small, this is a great package for chocolates, small gifts, or pen sets — it can be decorated for a vertical or a horizontal presentation. The package is made from one folded piece with an interlocking tab closure. Windows also work well in this design. Follow the instructions on pages 24 and 25 for cutting and scoring the template, then fold in and glue the side tabs.

Pattern can be found on page 124.

Pictured above, top to bottom:

• **Berry Package** used a decorative paper napkin with strawberry motifs fused to card paper. Artificial raspberries and blackberries, silk leaves, raffia, and a hand-lettered sticker complete the package.

• **Jingle Bell Package** creates a holiday look with green paper, stickers, red rosebuds and a gold bullion bow. Another sticker adorns a coordinating gift card.

• The smaller **Greetings Package** is festive but understated. Decorations include a bee charm and artificial greenery.

Pictured on the opposite page, clockwise from top left:

• **Raspberry Package** is a tall box cut from decorative paper with a circular window, which was covered with a clear plastic sheet and natural mesh. Silk leaves and stickers were glued on the front panel; raffia and artificial berries are accents.

82

- **Egyptian-inspired Package** uses tissue paper laminated to card paper with the faux leather technique. A piece of gold ribbon, polymer clay seal, and a label provide finishing touches.

- The **Dream Package** shows how different paper and embellishments can give a different effect. The matching gift card can be tucked into the ribbon on the back panel.

Fold-over Package

These packages are a breeze to construct, and they are economical when you need lots of packages. The idea is simple – card weight paper is folded over a cellophane bag filled with an herb blend, bath salts, tea blends, or any small gift that can be placed in a bag.

Here's How

1. Cut a strip of card paper a little wider than the bag you are going to use inside. (Fig. 1) For larger bags, glue two card paper strips together to form a strip long enough to fold over the bag.

2. Score and fold the strip in half. (Fig. 2)

3. Form the gusset by folding again in the middle, 1/2" to 1-1/2" away from the first fold. (Fig. 3) The size of the gusset depends on what's in the bag; for larger bags, you need a larger gusset.

4. Place the bag inside the folded paper strip, fold over the flap, and staple all layers together to hold. (Fig. 4) If you're giving a culinary gift that requires a recipe, print the recipe on a label or a piece of paper and glue it to the inside panel before inserting the bag.

5. Decorate the package with labels, stickers, seals, charms, and/or ribbon. (Fig. 5)

Fig. 1

Fig. 2

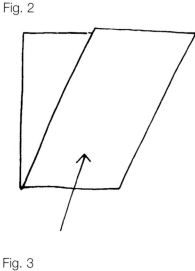

Fig. 3

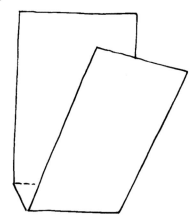

Fig. 4

Fig. 5

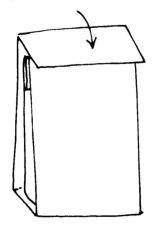

Pictured above:
The three fold-over packages standing up, left to right, show flap variations and different ways to decorate them with ribbons, stickers, and paper cutouts.

The **Dill Fold-over Package** is decorated with a twig, some raffia, and stamped polymer clay leaf, which also serves as the label.

Variations to the fold-over package include the matchbook style package, *pictured above on the right and on the opposite page,* and the fold-over door sign, *pictured above left.* • The **Matchbook** style is similar to the basic fold-over package, but is constructed so the front panel tucks under a bottom flap. It is an excellent package for jewelry attached to a card – you can staple the card inside the folded package.

• The **Door Sign Package** is made from a die-cut paper door sign. Decorate the door sign by laminating it with decorative paper, painting, or applying stickers, then simply fold the sign in half and staple a bag inside. (This idea is courtesy of Jacqueline Bartels, a representative of the Magenta Stamp Company, which manufactured the stamp used to decorate the example.)

Teabag-style Package

For this package, the paper is folded in thirds and forms a pocket. (The shape reminds me of "flow-through" type teabags – hence the name.) It is a good design for individual tea and coffee blends, scented bath salts, and other small gifts. If you're placing a culinary treat in the package, line the package before you construct it by laminating freezer paper to the paper that will be used on the outside. I especially like to use soft handmade paper to make this package.

Here's How

1. Fold the paper into thirds lengthwise. (Fig. 1)

2. Fold in half (Fig. 2a) and then again 1" away from the first fold (Fig. 2b) to form the gusset.

3. Unfold the paper and place glue as indicated in Fig. 3.

4. Refold the sachet and press to adhere well. Place the product inside the pouches formed on each side. (Fig. 4)

5. Fold over the flap and trim the edges. Staple or punch a hole through all the layers and add a brad to hold. (Fig. 5)

6. Add a label and stickers to decorate the front of the sachet.

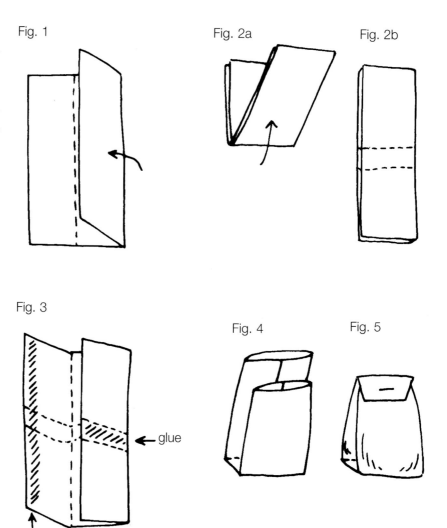

Fig. 1

Fig. 2a

Fig. 2b

Fig. 3

← glue

glue

Fig. 4

Fig. 5

Envelope Pouch

This quick and easy pouch can be made to wrap any gift that can be placed in an envelope, such as jewelry, gift certificates, cash, or checks. The pouch is created from a single piece of paper and does not require gluing. I like to use handmade paper that has been trimmed with gold paper or that has a gold embossed edge. The faux leather technique can be used to make nice leather-like pouches.

The example shows how to cover an envelope 4" x 5-1/4" with an 8-1/2" x 11" sheet of paper.

Here's How

1. Trim the paper to 8" x 10".

2. Place the envelope on the middle of the paper at an angle. (Fig. 1)

3. Fold up two opposite corners of the paper flush with the envelope to form the sides. (Fig. 2) Remove the envelope. Press the folds firmly. Unfold.

4. Replace the envelope. Fold up the bottom. Remove the envelope. Press the folds firmly. Unfold.

5. Decorate the envelope.

6. Replace the envelope (with the gift inside), fold up the bottom of the package, then fold in the sides to wrap the envelope. (Fig. 3)

7. Close the pouch with a sticker or self-adhesive label, then add a greeting or additional decorations, such as charms or ribbon.

Fig. 1

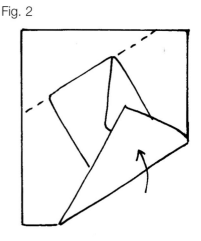

Fig. 2

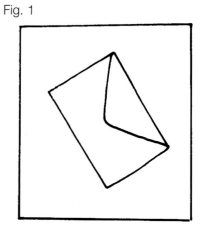

Fig. 3

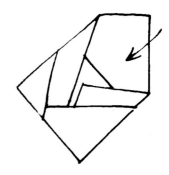

Traditional Christmas Crackers

Christmas Crackers are an English holiday tradition that dates to the Victorian era. The tubes are filled with a small gift, handmade ornament, goofy tissue paper hats (we wear them during Christmas dinner), or a joke or inspirational saying printed on a piece of paper. When everyone sits down for dinner, you cross your arms and grasp the end of your banger in the tube and the person's next to you on the other side. When you are all organized, everyone pulls on the bangers to make the crackers crack. Sometimes these bangers (which actually are friction strips) can be very loud! Everyone rips open their crackers and takes a turn reading the joke or saying inside.

They are a Christmas tradition with our family and a popular bazaar item in our area – maybe you'll adopt them as a tradition in your family.

You'll Need (to make one cracker)

3 cardboard tubes, one 4" long and two 2" long

1 cracker banger

3 sheets tissue paper, 12" x 6"

1 piece handmade paper 8" x 6"

2 pieces decorative paper, one 4" x 6" and one 3" x 6"

Heavy thread or light cording

Embellishments

For inside: A small gift or ornament or tissue paper hat, plus a joke or riddle written on a piece of paper

Fig. 1 - Banger Placement

The banger is placed under the middle tube and folded into the center of the smaller tubes.

Here's How

1. Place the present and joke inside the 4" tube.
2. Stack the sheets of tissue paper. Lay the banger along the edge of the evenly stacked tissue paper pieces; put the filled tube over the banger.
3. Place the two short tubes at each end of the larger tube, 1-1/2" away. Bend the banger to fit inside shorter tubes. See Fig. 1.
4. When everything is evenly spaced and centered, roll up the tissue paper around the cardboard tubes. Secure with tape.
5. Wrap the other pieces of paper around the tube, starting with the largest piece. Secure each with tape.
6. Tie threads between the tubes, pulling gently to close. When tight, knot and cut the ends. Push short tubes inward to tidy up the package.
7. Decorate the outside of the cracker with ribbon, silk greenery, stickers, or seals that coordinate with your paper choice.
8. Remove the two short tubes. (Keep them for making the next cracker.) With scissors, cut slits in the tissue paper ends.

Pictured at right:

Christmas crackers are decorated with ribbons and polymer clay seals. The cracker idea can also be used to make a vertical gift package for any time of year. You don't need a banger; just push the tissue inside the tube on one end. Here, a sign with a greeting is glued to a piece of wire and placed in the cracker.

Making Gift Bags

GIFT BAGS ARE AN INCREASINGLY POPULAR ALTERNATIVE for wrapping gifts of all sizes. Blank paper gift bags are easy to find and fun to decorate, and making your own is easy.

Patterns for making gift bags appear on pages 125 and 126. To make bags, follow the instructions in the Basic Techniques section for cutting and scoring, then assemble the bags by folding in and gluing the side and bottom tabs.

After a gift is placed in a bag, the top can be held closed with ribbon or cord laced through punched holes or eyelets, with clips, or with buttons. Or you can leave the top of the bag open and conceal the contents with tissue or shredded colored paper.

Fabric-Covered Bags

Fabric-covered bags are strong and can be recycled for many gift exchanges. These bags were made from paper fused with cotton fabric using iron-on fusible webbing. The handles are cut from scraps that are left over after you cut out the bag.

You can use the same fabric to make a bag's handle or a coordinating one, as was done here. Use a glue gun to glue the handles and a decorative button to the top of the bag. A miniature clothespin was glued on the front panel and holds a paper gift card.

Tall Gift Bag

This package is cut in one piece. Wire clips, labels, brads, and cording can be used to close this slender design. Follow the instructions in the Basic Techniques section for cutting and scoring the paper, then fold in and glue the side and bottom tabs.

These holiday-theme bags were fashioned from dark green and red card paper. Simple gold designs were added to the front panel with a gold paint pen before the bag was assembled. The matching gift tags were rubber-stamped, punched, and threaded through with gold elastic cord – a closure and tag in one.

Quick Bag Favors

This is a quick, economical way to make lots of favors for a party or special event. Clear dimensional fabric paint is used to glue beads and buttons on small, colorful paper bags. Fabric paint gives a strong hold and adds a touch of glitter – but test it first to make sure it won't seep through the bags. (If it does, use a piece of cardboard inside the bag while the paint dries.) Choose plastic beads and buttons that complement your party theme. Arrange them and glue with clear paint, let dry overnight, then embellish with a gel pen. Cut the tops with decorative-edge scissors, fold over, and secure with swirl wire clips. If you write the name of each guest on a bag, you can use them as place cards at the table. You could also punch two holes, thread ribbon through the holes, and tie in a bow to hold a bag closed.

La Petite Purse

This clever bag design is super easy and a great way to use one-of-a-kind buttons. You can hang the petite purses from their handles or use them as favors for a ladies' tea or a teen girl's party.

I think the best-looking purses are made with small metallic bags, but you could also use plain paper bags decorated with stamps or sponging. Thanks to Jacqueline Bartels of Magenta Stamps for another great idea.

Pictured opposite: Petite purses in a variety of sizes.

Instructions follow on page 100.

La Petite Purse

continued from page 98

Here's How

1. Place the items in the bag.

2. Fold the top of the bag to a point. (Fig. 1) Crease well with a bone folder.

3. Glue a loop of ribbon or cord right under the fold. (Fig. 2)

4. Fold the bag so the folded point is at the bottom front of the bag. Glue with a glue gun to hold. Add a button or charm to the front of your bag to embellish. (Fig. 3)

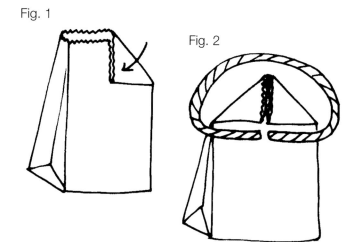

Fig. 1

Fig. 2

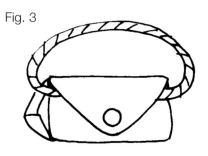

Fig. 3

Bag Toppers

Bag toppers are a great way to dress up an ordinary paper bag. You can find die-cut toppers ready to decorate and use, or you can make your own from just about any kind of paper.

Here's How

1. Use a circle template or a plate with a diameter the same measurement as the top of the bag to make a circle pattern.

2. Use the pattern to trace the circle on decorative paper. Embellish as you like, using decorative-edge scissors, punches, markers, or paint.

3. Fold down the top of the bag. Fold the bag topper in half and place it over the bag.

4. Punch two holes, thread through a piece of ribbon, and tie in a bow. (If adding a gift tag, thread it on the ribbon before making the bow.)

Pictured opposite: Three festive bags in silver, gold, and white sport toppers with snowflake motifs. The bag at upper right is held closed by an artificial berry branch threaded through the punched holes. A little bee sticker is the finishing touch.

Accordion Top Bag

Making an accordion top is another easy way to make an attractive package from a plain bag. You can decorate plain brown bags with rubber stamps, stencils, sponged or block printed motifs, or you can use patterned bags.

Here's How

1. Place the gift in the bag.

2. Starting at the top, fold the top of the bag back and forth, like a fan. (How many folds you make depends on how full the bag is.) Hold the pleats with a large paper clip while you complete the next steps.

3. Locate the center of your fold with a ruler. Mark, then punch a hole in the center going through all the folds. (You may be able to punch through only two folds at a time.)

4. Thread cord or ribbon through the hole and tie in a bow. Remove the paper clip.

5. Bring the ends of the first two folds together and hold with the large paper clip. (You could staple or glue them at this point, but the paper clip holds well – and it's easy for the recipient to open the gift.)

6. Decorate the front of the bag with a sticker.

Pictured opposite: Combining red and green gives a holiday look. The stickers were made by writing with a gold pen on colorful paper, trimming with scissors, and using an adhesive application machine.

Beyond Paper

OTHER SIMPLE AND FUN PACKAGES CAN BE CREATED from materials other than paper, such as metal, plastic, terra cotta, and fabrics of all kinds. Many of these surfaces are available for sale, ready for your decorative treatments. Others, such as fabric bags, can be constructed of yard goods by anyone with minimal sewing skills (or even with fabric glue).

Metal Packages

Plain metal tins in a variety of shapes can be bought at packaging and container outlets, ready to decorate. Here, I used a small paint tin, a round tin, and a CD tin. I made the labels with green paper and did the lettering with a silver paint pen. I used an adhesive application machine to turn the paper labels into stickers. You could also use spray adhesive; the labels tend to fall off when a glue stick is used.

Pictured clockwise from top left:

• The **Tea Tin** is trimmed with copper tape. Tea-themed silver charms are glued on the top, and the tin holds a favorite tea blend.

• The **Music Tin** has an embossed copper tag threaded on metallic cord. The holes of the tag were reinforced with eyelets (if you don't do this, the sharp edge will cut through the cord).

• The **Daisy Tin**, which is also trimmed with copper tape, is decorated with posies punched from thin aluminum sheets and mounted on paper. Painted eyelets (as flower centers) and curled wire tendrils were added before gluing the flowers to magnets.

105

The label on the **Creative Quotes Tin** was made in the same manner as the gift inside. I printed the quotes on paper and cut them out, using a personal shape cutter and shape template. Then I ran the paper pieces through an adhesive application machine with the laminate/magnet cartridge, which instantly turns the paper pieces into beautiful magnets for the refrigerator or filing cabinet. The tin is closed with a loop of metallic elastic cord.

Plastic Containers

Plastic is a great medium for packages; it is practical and inexpensive. My favorite way to decorate plastic is with dimensional fabric paints. Plastic CD containers, purses, gift bags, bottles, and boxes all look great with this bright paint technique.

Dimensional paint holds up very well in the bathroom, making it a wonderful way to decorate containers to hold fragrant bath oils, bubble bath, or bath salts. You can also sprinkle tiny glass marbles on wet dimensional paint for a stunning beaded effect, as shown on the bottle and bath salts containers in the photo.

Keep the dimensional paint designs simple, such as stars or swirls or small flowers grouped together. (See the opposite page for patterns for dimensional paint designs.)

Patterns

Happy

Fabric Bags & Pouches

You can make your own simple fabric bags and pouches or purchase plain ones and decorate them. Bags are great packages – they can be made to fit just about any gift and because they can be re-used they are a gift themselves. To decorate the bags on these two pages, I used dimensional fabric paint. For best results, keep the designs simple and remember to place a sheet of wax paper into the bag before applying the paint or you will glue the front and back of the bag together.

Purchased muslin bags, *pictured left,* are decorated with seashore motifs. Fabric glue was squeezed on the bags in designs and shells, colored sand, and crushed coral were sprinkled on the wet paint for a natural look. The string ties that came with the bags were replaced with raffia. The large bag has a wooden button and a hook-and-loop closure.

Bags made from sheer fabric, *pictured on the opposite page,* are decorated with paint, silk flowers, and beads. The green sheer bag, *top left,* was covered with individual purple hydrangea blossoms (cut from a cluster) that were attached with a glue gun. A drop of gold fabric paint makes the center of each flower sparkle; a silk leaf was added to the bag top to finish. For a lavish, sparking effect, use tiny glass marbles attached with fabric paint. The sheer bag, *center,* has simple designs repeated in two colors. It's closed with a simple bow of narrow metallic ribbon. The golden bag, *top right,* is monogrammed with tiny marbles. The ends of the letters are embellished with faceted jewels (also glued with fabric paint), and jewels are attached at the ends of the satin-ribbon drawstrings.

Cellophane Wrapping

Wrapping packages in cellophane is an easy, quick way to give a special, finished appearance, and it's often the best way to unify a multi-item gift. Look for large rolls of cellophane in card shops and craft stores.

Painted clay pots, small boxes, compact discs, and books are easy to wrap with cellophane and create a beautiful presentation.

Here's How
1. Cut a square piece of cellophane about four times the height of the gifts. Place the gift(s) in the center of the cellophane.
2. Bring up two opposite sides to the top, then gather up the rest of the cellophane to the top and secure with a twist tie.
3. Smooth the cellophane on top and trim at an angle.
4. Add ribbon or fabric bows, gift tags, and other embellishments.

The **Olive Branch Gift** package was created by placing two quick boxes on a base before wrapping with the cellophane. (The base is a piece of mat board covered with matching paper – you also could use a book or a wrapped CD for the base.) Add a gold bow, an artificial olive branch, and a matching gift card.

For the **Once Upon a Time Gift**, a number of small gifts are wrapped together. A CD of lullabies is wrapped with baby-theme paper and used as the base for the boxes. Square boxes are decorated with coordinating paper and decorated with square panels, stickers, and letters. A shape template and cutter were used to make the positive and negative paper letters. The top is tied with a large blue tulle bow. A matching gift card finishes the presentation.

Terra Cotta Pot Packages

Clay pots make beautiful containers that are gifts in themselves. They are plentiful, easy to decorate, and very inexpensive.

The "jars" pictured at right are terra cotta pots with lids made from clay saucers with wooden knobs. To duplicate the look, basecoat with acrylic paints and let dry. Sketch simple designs with a chalk pencil and paint with gold metallic acrylic paint. When dry, sand the pots with medium grit sandpaper for a distressed look, wipe away the dust, and finish with a coat of varnish. They're now ready to fill with cellophane bags of home baked goodies, candles, or potpourri.

To make sure the knobs do not pull off, drill a hole in the center of the saucer and attach the knob with a wood screw. Add a little white glue around the screw to make it secure.

The clay pots, *pictured above,* are decorated with polymer clay that was impressed with alphabet rubber stamps and real leaves from the garden. To create the appearance of natural stone, mix translucent clay with spices such as chili powder or paprika for color. Form the labels and collars right on the pots and bake according to the manufacturer's directions. After baking, test the polymer clay pieces to be sure they are secure. (You may need to use white glue to adhere them permanently.)

Fill cellophane bags with goodies and place them in the pots. Tie the bags with raffia and add a leaf label made from polymer clay. You can impress the recipient's name with alphabet stamps before baking.

Raffia Bee Pattern

Christmas Lights Pattern

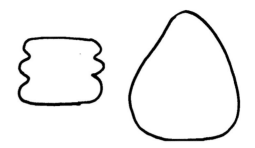

Wire Clips Patterns

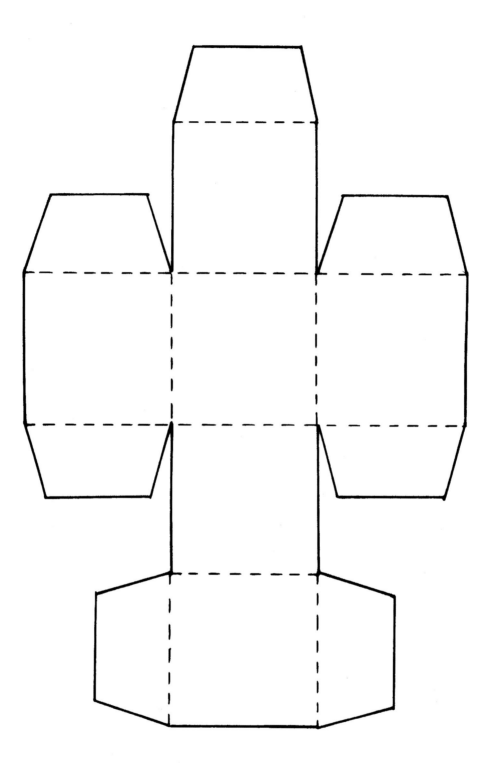

Pyramid Box Pattern

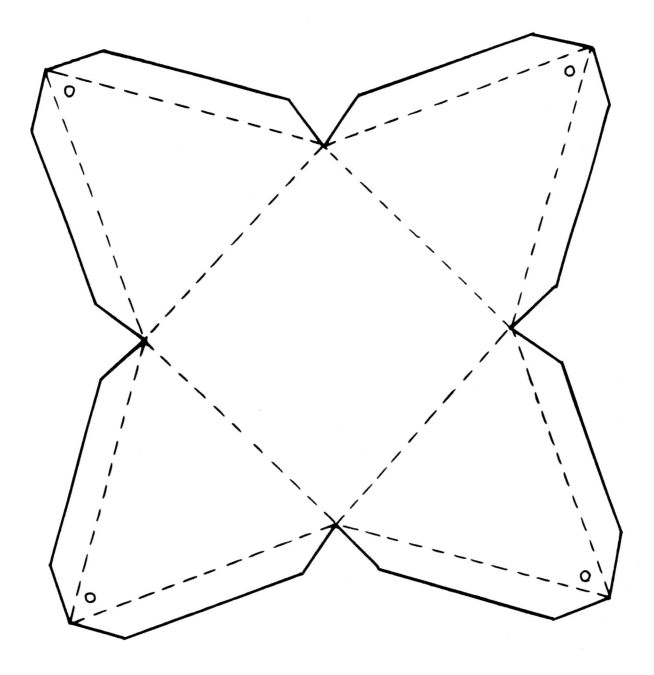

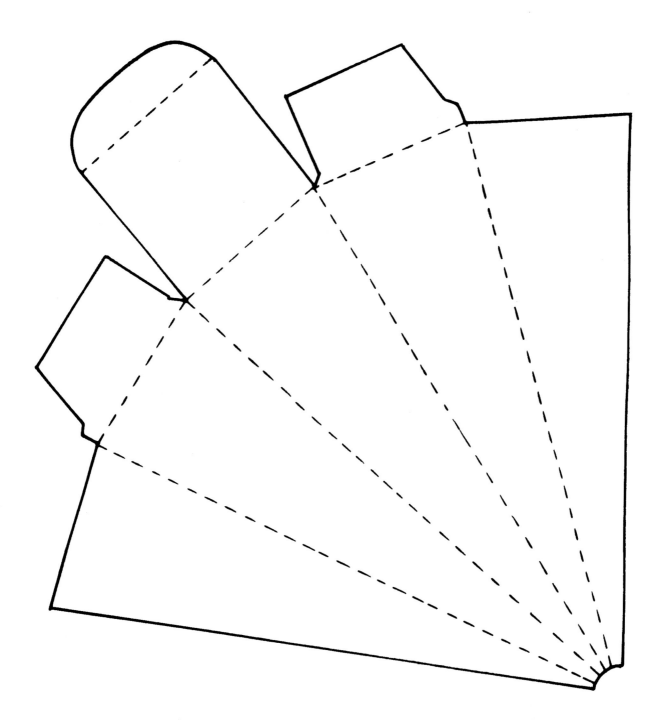

Pillow Pouch Pattern

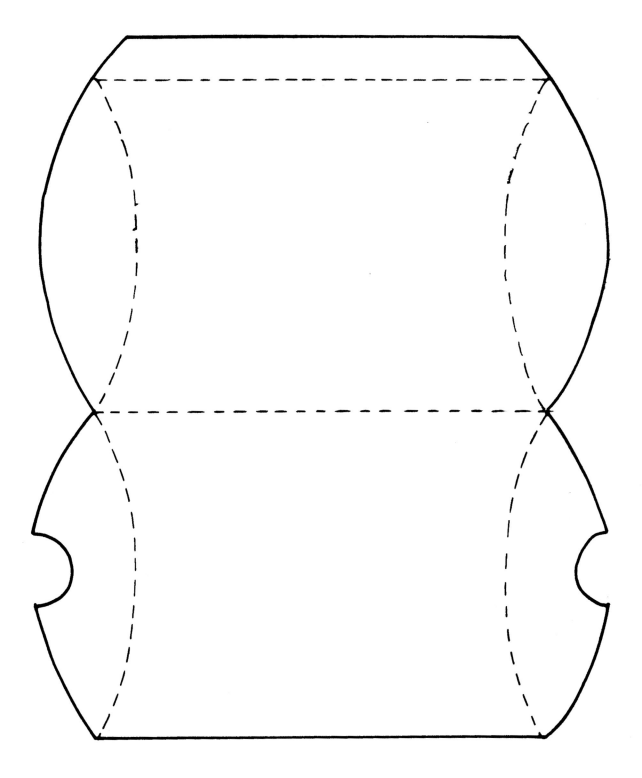

Interlocking Box Pattern

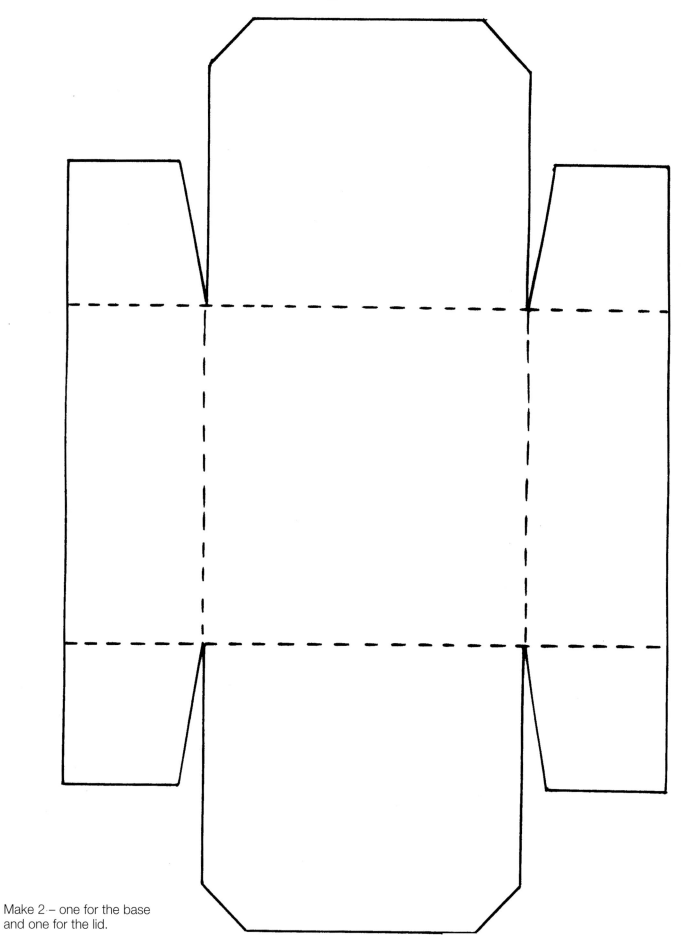

Make 2 – one for the base
and one for the lid.

Paper Purse Pattern

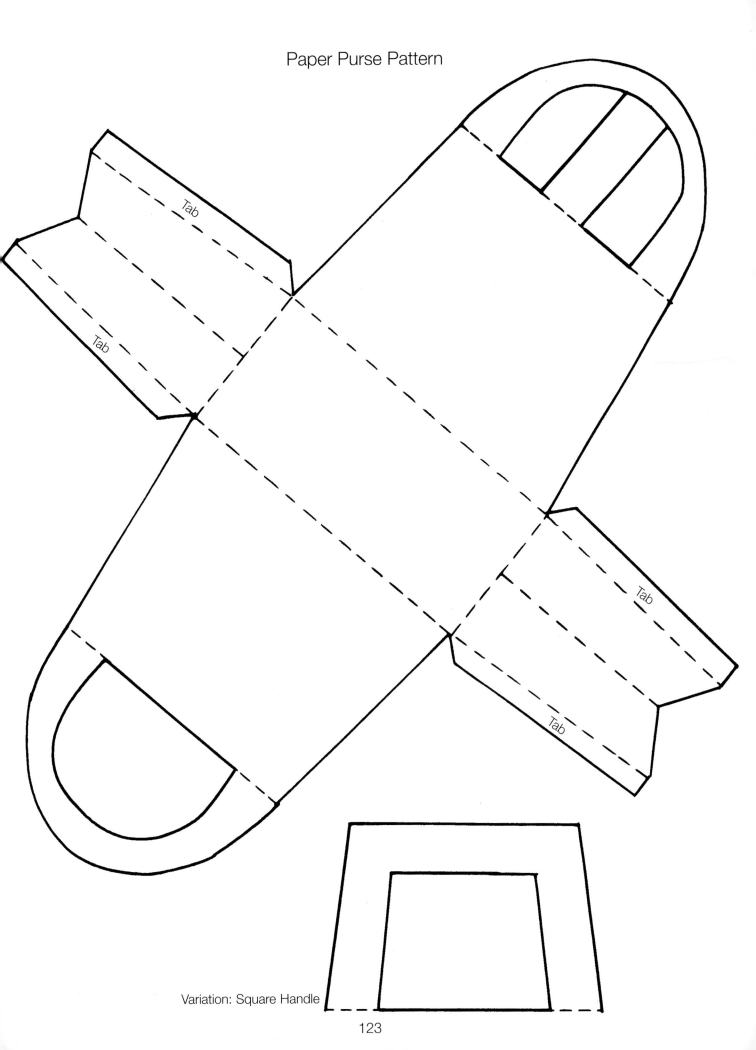

Tab

Tab

Tab

Tab

Variation: Square Handle

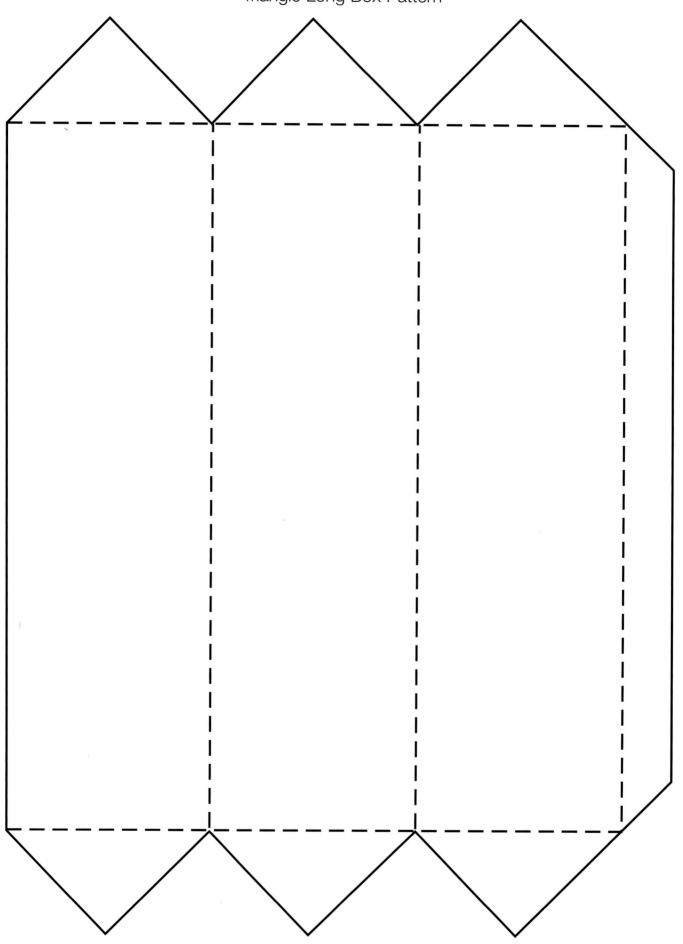

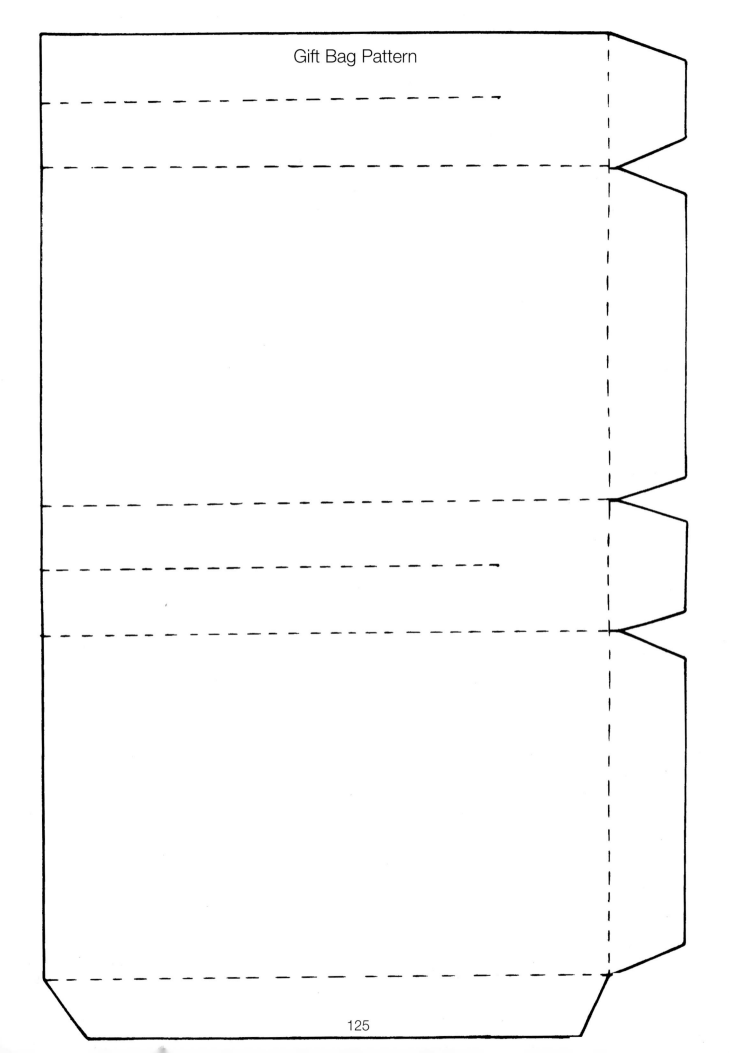

Gift Bag Pattern

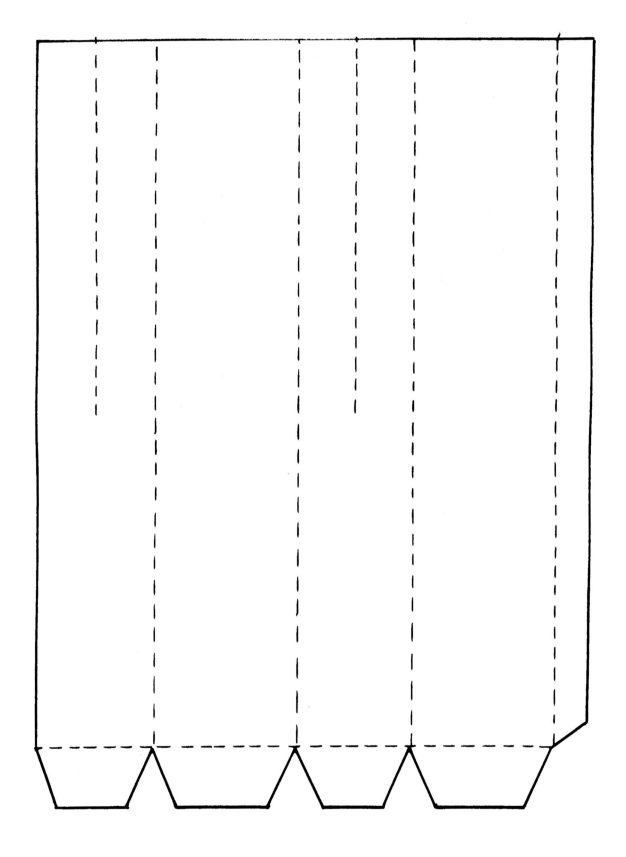

Metric Conversion Chart

Inches to Millimeters and Centimeters

Inches	MM	CM
1/8	3	.3
1/4	6	.6
3/8	10	1.0
1/2	13	1.3
5/8	16	1.6
3/4	19	1.9
7/8	22	2.2
1	25	2.5
1-1/4	32	3.2
1-1/2	38	3.8
1-3/4	44	4.4
2	51	5.1
3	76	7.6
4	102	10.2
5	127	12.7
6	152	15.2
7	178	17.8
8	203	20.3
9	229	22.9
10	254	25.4
11	279	27.9
12	305	30.5

Yards to Meters

Yards	Meters
1/8	.11
1/4	.23
3/8	.34
1/2	.46
5/8	.57
3/4	.69
7/8	.80
1	.91
2	1.83
3	2.74
4	3.66
5	4.57
6	5.49
7	6.40
8	7.32
9	8.23
10	9.14

Index

A

Accordion top bag 102

Adhesives 10, 13, 17, 19, 20, 21, 35, 40, 48, 49, 60, 102, 105

Antiquing paper 30, 38

B

Bag toppers 100

Bags see ìGift bagsî

Block printing 29

Bottles 15

Box blanks 14, 28, 55, 68, 72

Boxes 15, 50, 52, 54, 56, 60, 63, 64, 66, 68, 70, 77, 82

C

Card stock (or paper) 12, 20, 25, 26, 27, 28, 34, 38, 51, 52, 55, 63, 65, 70, 73, 76, 77, 82, 83, 84, 96

Cardboard boxes 15

Cellophane wrapping 72, 84, 112, 113, 114, 116

Christmas crackers 92

Clay pots 15, 113, 114, 116

Clear plastic sheets 13, 72

Collapsible box 60

Column twist container 79

Cornucopia box 68, 70, 120

Cover a box 46, 48, 49

Crackers see ìChristmas crackersî

Cutting (technique) 24

Cutting tools 17

D

Decorating Materials 22

Decorative paper 12, 14, 15, 23, 28, 30, 31, 38, 40, 46, 48, 52, 56, 60, 66, 70, 72, 76, 80, 82, 92, 100

Decoupage 12, 17, 20, 26, 27, 30, 34, 46, 48, 65, 70

Die-cut packages 15

E

Envelope pouch 90

Equipment 16

F

Fabric 14, 15, 17, 20, 22, 23, 27, 36, 37, 49, 68, 95, 104, 110

Fabric paint 36, 37, 64, 65, 70, 97, 107, 108, 110

Faux leather 13, 20, 34, 83, 90

Fold over package 84, 85, 86

Folding (technique) 25

Folding tools 18

G

Gift bags 14, 94, 95, 96, 97, 102, 110, 125, 126

Glass beads 37

Gold leafing 35

Gluing (technique) 26

H

Handmade paper 12, 46, 48, 76, 88, 90, 92

I

Interlocking box, 77, 122

J

Jars 15, 114

L

Labels 12, 17, 20, 22, 30, 38, 41, 51, 84, 96, 105 116

Laminating (technique) 27

M

Mat board 13, 64, 65, 113

Match box 63

Materials 10

Metal packages 105

O

Origami box 56

P

Paper 11, 12, 13

Paper purse 78, 123

Papier mache boxes 15, 46

Parchment 13, 18, 25, 36, 70

Petite purse 98, 99

Photographs 13, 72

Pillow pouch 72, 121

Plastic containers 107

Pointed paper pouch 74, 75, 76

Polymer clay 23, 43, 46, 63, 66, 70, 77, 83, 85, 92, 116

Pouches 72, 74, 76, 90, 110

Pyramid box 66, 119

Q

Quick box 52

R

Rubber stamps 13, 32, 43, 55, 66, 98, 102, 116

S

Sandpaper 13, 66, 79, 114

Shaped boxes 64

Sponging 28, 98

Square box 54, 118

Stencil templates 15, 72

Stickers 40, 72, 78, 79, 82, 84, 88, 92, 102, 105, 113

Suede paper 13, 46, 48, 78

T

Tags 38, 41, 44, 96, 113

Tea bag-style package 88

Templates 51

Terra cotta pot packages, see "Clay pots"

Tissue paper 13, 27, 30, 34, 83, 92

Triangle long box 82, 124

V

Vellum 13, 18, 25, 70, 72

W

Wire clips 23 42, 80, 96, 97